THAT AMAZING
PLACE

THAT AMAZING
PLACE

A Bible-Lands
Trivia Challenge

John Hudson Tiner

BARBOUR
PUBLISHING

THIS BOOK IS DEDICATED TO
CHRISTIAN WAYNE STEPHENS.

© 2011 by Barbour Publishing, Inc.

ISBN 978-1-60260-897-9

All scripture quotations are taken from the King James Version of the Bible.

Published by Barbour Publishing, Inc., P.O. Box 719, Uhrichsville, Ohio 44683 www.barbourbooks.com

Our mission is to publish and distribute inspirational products offering exceptional value and biblical encouragement to the masses.

ecpa Member of the
Evangelical Christian
Publishers Association

Printed in the United States of America.

CONTENTS

Starting Line Instructions. 9

Leg 1:   A City about Six Miles from
         Jerusalem 13

Leg 2:   One of the Most Frequently
         Mentioned Locations in the
         Bible. 21

Leg 3:   The River where John the Baptist
         Preached. 29

Leg 4:   A City on the Northeastern Shore
         of the Sea of Galilee. 37

Leg 5:   The Town where Jesus Did His First
         Miracle. 45

Leg 6:   The Well where Jesus Spoke to the
         Woman. 53

Leg 7:   Jesus Lived Here for Most of His
         Life. 61

Leg 8:   Apostles Made Their Living Fishing
         in the Lake. 69

Leg 9:   The Central Building of Their
         Worship 77

Leg 10: Joshua's Army Followed God's Plan
         for Taking the City. 85

Leg 11: A Small Village on the Mount of
Olives 93

Leg 12: The Name of the Garden Means
"Oil Press" .101

Leg 13: A Road where Jesus Walked and
Talked with Two Disciples 109

Leg 14: A Lame Man Sat at a Gate to the
Temple 117

Leg 15: The City where Simon the Sorcerer
Lived 125

Leg 16: The Region where Samson Toppled
the Temple of Dagon 133

Leg 17: One of the Oldest and Most
Important Harbors of Ancient
Times 141

Leg 18: The City where Cornelius the
Centurion Had a Vision 149

Leg 19: A City where Saul Planned to Take
Christians Captive 157

Leg 20: In This City, Disciples of Jesus Were
Called by a New Name 165

Leg 21: An Island That Is the Birthplace of
Barnabas 173

Leg 22: A City where Paul Was Well
Received at First...............181

Leg 23: In This City, Paul Preached to a
Group of Women..............189

Leg 24: The Mob Carried the Home's
Owner before the Rulers of
the City 197

Leg 25: Paul Was Asked to Come to the
Areopagus 205

Leg 26: Here, Paul Met Two People—
Husband and Wife—Who Became
His Friends..................213

Leg 27: In This City, Some Jewish Exorcists
Tried to Drive Out Evil Spirits ...221

Leg 28: On This Island, the Inhabitants
Watched Closely after a Serpent
Bit Paul 229

Leg 29: This Is the City where Paul Was to
Stand Trial..................237

Leg 30: An Isle Mentioned in the Last
Book of the New Testament......245

STARTING LINE INSTRUCTIONS

Welcome to *That Amazing Place*, an exciting and challenging race through the sights and sounds of faraway Bible towns and locations. In this journey of a lifetime, you'll meet the local people and learn about the places where Jesus and the early disciples lived and taught. You'll race to historic places that in many cases are still occupied today. Each leg is anchored by an actual location where important events took place in the Bible. Racing from one leg to the next will test your Bible knowledge.

Tracing out these ancient routes will awaken an appreciation for the adventures—and the dangers—the early believers faced. You'll escape with Joseph and his family from the murderous intent of Herod. You'll travel a road noted for thieves that attack unwary travelers. You'll experience a terrific storm at sea, and you'll react in dismay as an angry mob threatens those speaking for Jesus.

But other destinations illustrate the delights of daily life in Bible times. You'll enjoy a small-town wedding celebration. After a long, dry, and dusty hike, you'll be refreshed with cool water from a hand-dug well. You'll pause to meditate in an olive grove near Jerusalem. You'll search out a small village in the hill country of Galilee and follow roads to a thriving metropolis at the heart of the Roman Empire.

But more important than the physical routes of the Christian pioneers is the *spiritual* journey that brings you into a closer relationship with the Savior. Your scores on the legs may not be as you would want them to be—if so, polish your knowledge by looking up the verse references given with the answers. They'll be a guide to drawing more closely to the essential points of the gospel.

As with the travels in this book, life's journey will throw speed bumps, roadblocks, and choices along your way. But God can work wonders in any place. Have faith in Him and receive a rich blessing, regardless of your circumstances or your place in the world. Enjoy *That Amazing Place*.

Now it is time to start your amazing adventure.

GET READY.
GET SET.
GO!

CHECKING IN

12–15 correct—You're the first to arrive!

8–11 correct—You have a substantial lead over the rest of the teams.

4–7 correct—You must have hit a speed bump that slowed you down. Refer to your way-markers in scripture to get back on course. Scramble to find your way to the next pit stop.

0–3 correct—You must have taken a wrong turn along the way and come in last. I'm happy to tell you this is a non-elimination leg. Review your answers and race to the next leg to make up lost time. Search more diligently for the route markers—Bible verses that show the road to salvation. Remember the loving Father will help those finish the race who are determined to remain faithful.

Note:
The answers for each leg follow the final question of that leg.

LEG 1

Your race 'round Bible lands begins now. Open the clue box to discover where you are going.

CLUE BOX:

In this leg, you will travel to a city about six miles from Jerusalem. The city is mentioned in the Old Testament in Genesis 35:19–20 as the site where Rachel, wife of Jacob, was buried. It is called the city of David, and more importantly it is the birthplace of the King of Kings.

Your destination is _____.

At Bethlehem, Rachel gave birth to Jacob's youngest son, whom he named _____.

True or False: Rachel had two sons.

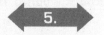

What prophet came to Bethlehem to anoint David as future king?

True or False: When David took food and water to his brothers from his father's farm at Bethlehem, they were facing a powerful enemy known as Barak, the Philistine champion from Gath.

Why did Naomi leave Bethlehem?

a. Hebrew women were being persecuted.
b. She could not find a husband.
c. She married a foreigner.
d. There was a famine.

Ruth was from what region?

    a. Galilee
    b. Moab
    c. Nineveh
    d. Syria

"And Ruth said, Intreat me not to leave thee, or to return from following after thee: for whither thou goest, I will go; and where thou lodgest, I will lodge: thy _____ shall be my _____, and thy _____ my _____."

At the time of Jesus' birth, which Caesar ordered the whole world to be taxed?

True or False: Joseph, the husband of Mary, was of the lineage of David.

Is Bethlehem in Galilee or Judea?

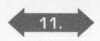

Who were the first to come see baby Jesus?

a.   Anna and Simeon at His presentation at
     the temple
b.   officers of Herod's court
c.   shepherds
d.   wise men

The wise men came to Jerusalem from:

a.   the east
b.   the west

How did Herod learn that the "King of the Jews"
would be born in Bethlehem?

a.   from an angel in a dream at night
b.   from his soothsayers
c.   from the chief priests and scribes who
     consulted scripture
d.   from his men who secretly followed the
     wise men

True or False: When Herod learned that Jesus would be born in Bethlehem, he hid that information from the wise men.

How were the wise men warned not to return to Herod?

LEG 1
ANSWERS

Bethlehem

1. Benjamin (Genesis 35:18)
2. True; Joseph and Benjamin (Genesis 35:24)
3. Samuel (1 Samuel 16:1, 13)
4. False; Goliath (1 Samuel 17:15, 23)
5. d. There was a famine (Ruth 1:1–2).
6. b. Moab (Ruth 1:4)
7. People, people, God, God (Ruth 1:16)
8. Augustus (Luke 2:1)
9. True (Luke 2:4)
10. Judea (Matthew 2:5)
11. c. shepherds (Luke 2:15–16)
12. a. east (Matthew 2:1)
13. c. from the chief priests and scribes (Matthew 2:3–5)
14. False; he told them to search for the child (Matthew 2:8).
15. In a dream (Matthew 2:12)

LEG 1
WELCOME TO THE CHECK-IN MAT

Congratulations upon finishing the first leg! Whether you are first to arrive or down in the pack, take a moment to rest and then get ready to race to the next place. It will be a long leg because the next location is far from Bethlehem. May God be with you.

But thou, Bethlehem Ephratah,
though thou be little among the thousands of Judah,
yet out of thee shall he come forth unto me
that is to be ruler in Israel;
whose goings forth have been
from of old, from everlasting.
MICAH 5:2

LEG 2

Simple shepherds and sophisticated wise men came to worship Jesus. But Joseph was warned that King Herod sought to destroy the young child. Joseph took the boy far from Bethlehem. Read the clue to learn his, and your, next destination.

CLUE BOX:

As a place and a nation, your goal is one of the most frequently mentioned locations in the Bible, occurring more than six hundred times. It's the country that figures into Bible stories from Genesis to the Gospel of Matthew. It is where Abram told a lie about his wife, where a son of Jacob was sold into slavery, where baby Moses slept in a floating basket, and where Jesus and His family escaped the murderous intent of King Herod.

Make your way to the country of _____.

When Abram and his wife, Sarai, traveled to Egypt, why did Abram let Pharaoh believe that Sarai was his sister?

What did God bring upon Pharaoh's house because of Abram's lie?

    a.   a great famine
    b.   death of his princes
    c.   great plagues
    d.   drying up of the Nile

True or False: When Pharaoh learned that Sarai was Abram's wife, he offered Abram a parcel of land to be his home.

When the sons of Jacob saw their brother, Joseph, approaching, they said, "Behold, this _____ cometh."

The one who counseled against killing Joseph was:

a. Benjamin
b. Reuben

The brothers stripped Joseph of what article of clothing before casting him into a pit?

What did his brothers receive when they sold Joseph to the Ishmeelites?

a. a donkey on which no one had ridden
b. a kid of goats
c. spices of balm and myrrh
d. twenty pieces of silver

8.

How can Joseph's master Potiphar be described?

a. a captain of the guard
b. an Egyptian
c. an officer of Pharaoh
d. all of the above

Though Joseph served Potiphar well, who told lies that caused him to be put into prison?

How did the daughter of Pharaoh come to discover baby Moses in the river of Egypt?

Jesus' travels from Egypt fulfilled what prophecy?

    a.   A prince shall come out of Egypt.
    b.   Out of Egypt have I called My Son.
    c.   He would pass through the Red Sea as by dry land.
    d.   The Son of man hath not where to lay His head.

In and around Bethlehem, Herod ordered the slaughter of all children of what age and under?

13.

"In Rama was there a voice heard, lamentation, and weeping, and great mourning, _____ weeping for her children, and would not be comforted, because they are not."

14.

What event allowed Joseph, Mary, and Jesus to leave Egypt?

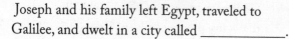

15.

Joseph and his family left Egypt, traveled to Galilee, and dwelt in a city called _____.

LEG 2
ANSWERS

Egypt

1. He feared the Egyptians would kill him so they could have her (Genesis 12:12–13).
2. c. great plagues (Genesis 12:17)
3. False; he sent Abram out of Egypt (Genesis 12:20, 13:1).
4. Dreamer (Genesis 37:19)
5. b. Reuben (Genesis 37:22)
6. Coat of many colors (Genesis 37:23)
7. d. twenty pieces of silver (Genesis 37:28)
8. d. all of the above (Genesis 39:1)
9. Potiphar's wife (Genesis 39:7–20)
10. She went down to wash herself (Exodus 2:5).
11. b. "Out of Egypt have I called my son" (Matthew 2:15).
12. Two years (Matthew 2:16)
13. Rachel (Matthew 2:18)
14. Herod's death (Matthew 2:19–20)
15. Nazareth (Matthew 2:23)

LEG 2
WELCOME TO THE CHECK-IN MAT

Ancient historians called Egypt a "gift of the Nile."
Egypt became a great empire despite being in the
heart of deserts. The four-thousand-mile long Nile
River continued to flow in the severest drought. All
along the fertile banks of the Nile arose impressive
cities, monuments, temples, and pyramids. In this
race through the amazing places of the Bible, you'll
next go to a small and short river that is as important
in its own way as the much longer Nile.

Our fathers understood not thy wonders in Egypt;
they remembered not the multitude of thy mercies;
but provoked him at the sea,
even at the Red sea.
PSALM 106:7

THAT AMAZING
PLACE

LEG 3

Scripture is silent about most of the early life of Jesus. The two times He is mentioned is as an eight-day-old child (Luke 2:21–22) and as a twelve-year-old (Luke 2:42). Both times He is in Jerusalem at the temple. But Jesus did not begin His public ministry in Jerusalem. Instead, He sought out a preacher who taught in the wilderness. Check the clue box for where you are traveling to next.

CLUE BOX:

Your next destination is the river where John the Baptist preached. Unlike the Nile, it is neither a great river in length nor in the volume of water it carries. However, many significant events in world history happened along its banks. When Abram gave Lot first choice of the land, Lot chose to live in the valley of this river (Genesis 13:10). By crossing it, the children of Israel entered the Promised Land. John the Baptist preached on its banks, and Jesus was baptized in its waters.

Make your way to the _____ River.

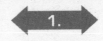

Lot chose the area near the Jordan River because it was well watered like what other land?

When Joshua and the children of Israel came to the Jordan, what did the Lord tell them to do to cross the river on dry land?

a. Joshua and Caleb were to stretch out their arms on either side of the river.
b. Joshua was to raise his staff.
c. The Levites carrying the Ark of the Covenant were to step into the water.
d. They were to wait for a dry wind from the west.

How many stones were removed from the Jordan River to make a monument?

Moses had given the inheritance to two-and-a-half tribes on the side of the Jordan River to the:

a. east
b. west

True or False: Elijah parted the Jordan River and crossed alone while Elisha watched from the other side.

After the appearance of the chariot of fire and the horses of fire, how did Elijah go up into heaven?

True or False: John the Baptist was preaching in the wilderness of Judea.

Where did Jesus come from to be baptized by John the Baptist?

    a. an unnamed city near Jerusalem
    b. Bethlehem of Judea
    c. Cana of Galilee
    d. Nazareth of Galilee

John the Baptist said, "I am the _____ of one crying in the wilderness."

John the Baptist ate locusts and _____
_____. (two words)

How did John the Baptist describe the Pharisees
and Sadducees?

    a.   generation of vipers
    b.   sons of perdition
    c.   swine
    d.   vultures

From what did John the Baptist say God could raise
up children of Abraham?

    a.   green shoots from dead roots
    b.   barren women
    c.   mustard seeds
    d.   stones

Who ruled as Caesar when Jesus was baptized?

    a. Claudius
    b. Julius
    c. Nero
    d. Tiberius

True or False: Pontius Pilate was the governor of Galilee when Jesus was baptized.

How did the Spirit of God descend on Jesus after His baptism?

LEG 3
ANSWERS

Jordan

1. Egypt (Genesis 13:10)
2. c. The Levites carrying the Ark of the Covenant were to step into the water (Joshua 3:13).
3. Twelve (Joshua 4:20)
4. a. east (Joshua 18:7)
5. False; they both went over (2 Kings 2:8).
6. By a whirlwind (2 Kings 2:11)
7. True (Matthew 3:1)
8. d. Nazareth of Galilee (Mark 1:9)
9. Voice (John 1:23)
10. Wild honey (Matthew 3:4)
11. a. generation of vipers (Luke 3:7)
12. d. stones (Matthew 3:9)
13. d. Tiberius (Luke 3:1)
14. False; Judea (Luke 3:1)
15. Like a dove (Mark 1:10)

LEG 3
WELCOME TO THE CHECK-IN MAT

Did you enjoy your race to the Jordan River? It is the destination of thousands of visitors each year. The little river is filled with history. It has been a river of dreams to millions of people through the centuries. The phrase "crossing the Jordan" has become a symbol of God's love. He gives a believer a peaceful home with Him for eternity.

Take a rest stop, discuss what you've learned with your fellow contestants, and get ready to race again. This time, you'll trace the Jordan River north to a fishing village on the Sea of Galilee.

Hear, O Israel:
Thou art to pass over Jordan this day,
to go in to possess nations greater
and mightier than thyself,
cities great and fenced up to heaven.
DEUTERONOMY 9:1

THAT AMAZING
PLACE

LEG 4

Your next destination is a city on the northeastern shore of the Sea of Galilee. The distance to it from where John preached is about eighty-five miles. But most Jewish travelers did not take the direct route. They traveled the road to Jericho, crossed over to the west side of the Jordan River, and then headed north through Berea. This added about thirty miles to the distance, but avoided Samaria and Samaritans with whom most Jews would have nothing to do. Check the clue box to find more details about the city of your destination.

CLUE BOX:

You race next to a city that became Jesus' base after He left Nazareth. In this seaside city, He called four fishermen as His disciples. Crowds came to hear Jesus teach. Four men showed their faith by making an opening in a roof so they could lower a sick man to be healed by Jesus.

Travel north to the seaside city of _____.

True or False: Jesus left Nazareth and dwelt in Capernaum.

True or False: The Gospel of Luke says that before calling Simon Peter and Andrew, Jesus spoke from a boat owned by Simon (Peter).

In calling Peter and Andrew, Jesus said, "Come ye after me, and I will make you to become _____ of men."

Peter and Andrew followed Jesus:

    a.   straightaway
    b.   after finding their father

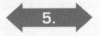

Who were the two sons of Zebedee that Jesus called as disciples?

What was the profession of Matthew (Levi) in Capernaum?

How did the centurion of Capernaum ask Jesus to heal his sick servant?

    a.   allow him to touch the hem of His garment
    b.   lay His hands on the servant
    c.   pray that the evil spirits would be removed
    d.   speak the word only

True or False: The Jewish leaders counseled Jesus to have nothing to do with the centurion because the centurion had tried to destroy their synagogue.

In speaking of the centurion, Jesus said, "Verily I say unto you, I have not found so great faith, no, not in _____."

Who was the relative of Simon Peter that Jesus healed?

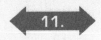

When Jesus taught in the synagogue at Capernaum, why were the listeners astonished at His doctrine?

    a. He taught as one with authority.
    b. He taught in statutes and judgments.
    c. He taught only in parables.
    d. He taught well into the night.

What statement did certain scribes object to when Jesus spoke to the man on the mat?

    a. "Arise, and take up thy bed and walk."
    b. "I have not seen such faith."
    c. "Son, thy sins be forgiven thee."
    d. "They that are whole have no need of the
        physician."

How many daughters did Jairus, a ruler of the synagogue, have?

When the woman with the issue of blood touched Jesus, He said, "Somebody hath touched me: for I perceive that _____ is gone out of me."

Jesus unfavorably compares Capernaum to what Old Testament city that God destroyed?

    a.   Antioch
    b.   Jericho
    c.   Sardis
    d.   Sodom

LEG 4
ANSWERS

Capernaum

1. True (Matthew 4:13)
2. True (Luke 5:3)
3. Fishers (Mark 1:17)
4. a. straightaway (Mark 1:18)
5. James and John (Mark 1:19–20)
6. Worked at the receipt of custom; that is, publican or tax collector (Mark 2:13–15)
7. d. speak the word only (Matthew 8:8)
8. False; he built the synagogue (Luke 7:4–5).
9. Israel (Matthew 8:10)
10. Simon Peter's wife's mother (Mark 1:30–31)
11. a. He taught as one with authority (Mark 1:22).
12. c. "Son, thy sins be forgiven thee" (Mark 2:5).
13. One (Luke 8:41–42)
14. Virtue (Luke 8:46)
15. d. Sodom (Matthew 11:23)

LEG 4
WELCOME TO THE CHECK-IN MAT

Count your correct answers and look on page seven to learn your standing. Did you manage to answer enough questions to have a comfortable lead? The last leg was an exhausting one. Even with the endurance of people in Bible times, the 115-mile walk to Capernaum from Jerusalem took about three days. The next leg of the race is much easier because it is only a few miles from Capernaum. It will be a lot of fun, too, because you are going to a wedding celebration.

The people that walked in darkness have seen a great light: they that dwell in the land of the shadow of death, upon them hath the light shined.
ISAIAH 9:2

THAT AMAZING
PLACE

LEG 5

Early in His ministry, Jesus, his mother, and the disciples were invited to a wedding feast in the town where you are going next. It was a small town about sixteen miles from Capernaum and a short distance from Nazareth. One of Jesus' disciples, Nathanael, was from this town. In the same general area is Gathhepher, the birthplace of the Old Testament prophet, Jonah (2 Kings 14:25). Read the clue box to identify your next destination.

CLUE BOX:

Travel to the town where Jesus did His first miracle—what the Gospel of John calls a "sign"—at the wedding feast in this town. It was a sign of His great power. His fame spread following the miracle. He traveled to Jerusalem and then traveled back through the town again. A nobleman from Capernaum found Him there and asked Jesus to heal his son who was dangerously ill.

Race from Capernaum to _____ in Galilee.

At the wedding, what problem did Jesus' mother bring to His attention?

Jesus said to His mother, "Woman, what have I to do with thee? mine _____ is not yet _____." (two words)

How many waterpots of stone did Jesus say to fill with water?

   a. two
   b. six
   c. twelve
   d. The number is not stated.

Who filled the waterpots?

   a.   bridegroom
   b.   governor of the feast
   c.   Jesus
   d.   servants

True or False: The governor of the feast reprimanded the bridegroom for saving the best wine until the last.

After the miracle at Cana, how did the disciples of Jesus react?

    a. They asked for the ability to do miracles.
    b. They asked, "What manner of man is this?"
    c. They believed on Him.
    d. They looked on Him with fear and trembling.

True or False: The disciple, Nathanael from Cana in Galilee, never saw Jesus after He arose.

Why did God direct Jonah to go to Nineveh?

Jonah instead took the road to _____ and found a ship going to Tarshish.

When Jonah finally entered Nineveh, how many days remained before God said it would be overthrown?

    a.   twelve
    b.   thirty
    c.   forty
    d.   seventy-seven

To show that they had repented, how did the people of Nineveh clothe themselves?

True or False: The efforts of the people did not prevail against the sure judgment of God.

How did Jonah react when he saw that the people of Nineveh had repented?

What benefit did the gourd provide for Jonah?

Rather than pity for the gourd after it died, God said He had a greater concern for what?

LEG 5
ANSWERS

Cana

1. They had no wine (John 2:3).
2. Hour, come (John 2:4)
3. b. six (John 2:6)
4. d. servants (John 2:5, 7)
5. False; spoke favorably (John 2:9–10)
6. c. They believed on Him (John 2:11).
7. False (John 21:1–2)
8. To cry against its great wickedness (Jonah 1:2)
9. Joppa (Jonah 1:3)
10. c. forty (Jonah 3:4)
11. They put on sackcloth (Jonah 3:6).
12. False; "God did it not" (Jonah 3:10).
13. He was very angry; he felt it better to die than to live (Jonah 4:1, 3).
14. It gave him shade (Jonah 4:6).
15. The people of the city of Nineveh (Jonah 4:10–11)

LEG 5
WELCOME TO THE CHECK-IN MAT

Did you find the correct city right away? Although a
small town, Cana in Galilee figured prominently in
the story of Jesus' public ministry. He did His first two
miracles (signs) in the little town. Even today, mar-
riage celebrations take place there, much as they did in
Bible times. They are multi-day events. By attending
the wedding celebration, Jesus showed His interest in
the events of everyday life. A wedding was a joyful occasion, just as Christianity is a joyful choice.

After a pleasant stop in Cana in Galilee, prepare
now to travel south into what many Jews of Jesus' day
considered a foreign country. They despised the people who lived there. Yet, Jesus not only traveled there,
but He engaged in conversation with them.

*Can a maid forget her ornaments,
or a bride her attire? yet my people have forgotten me
days without number.*
JEREMIAH 2:32

LEG 6

Now that you have rested from the wedding feast, it is time to set out to your next destination. You'll race to a water well outside the town of Sychar in Samaria. When Jesus came through the area, He spoke with a woman at the well. After carefully listening to Him and asking questions, she hurried into town to tell others to hear Him. Read the clue box to identify the name of the well.

Clue Box:

The well where Jesus spoke to the woman was named after a grandson of Abraham who bought the land. It was also near where Joshua of the Old Testament made his dramatic, "We will serve the Lord" speech.

Race to _____'s well outside the town of Sychar in Samaria.

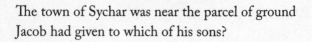

The town of Sychar was near the parcel of ground Jacob had given to which of his sons?

   a. Joseph
   b. Judah
   c. Reuben
   d. Simon

Why were the disciples not with Jesus when He met the woman at the well?

Why did the woman find it surprising that Jesus spoke with her?

"But whosoever drinketh of the water that I shall give him shall _____ thirst."

The woman said to Jesus, "Sir, I perceive that thou art a _____."

6.

Who said, "This is indeed the Christ, the Saviour of the world"?

a. a voice from heaven
b. the disciples when they returned from town
c. the Samaritans
d. the woman

7.

Where did the Samaritans worship God?

a. at the well
b. in Synagogues
c. in the mountains
d. in their homes

8.

True or False: Jesus told the woman, "Soon and very soon, all people shall worship in Jerusalem."

9.

"God is a _____: and they that worship him must worship him in _____ and in truth."

True or False: Jesus revealed directly to the woman that He was the Christ.

Jesus told His disciples that His "meat" was to do what?

    a.   "be about my father's business"
    b.   "change the customs which Moses gave us"
    c.   "deliver all things to my father"
    d.   "do the will of him that sent me"

After Jesus spoke to the Samaritans of Sychar, what did they do?

    a.   asked Him to tarry with them
    b.   asked Him to be a judge over them
    c.   asked Him to depart from them, a sinful people
    d.   asked Him to give them a miraculous sign

True or False: After Jesus spoke to the people of the Samaritan city directly, they said, "Now we believe."

Whose body was brought out of Egypt and buried in the parcel of land that Jacob had bought?

Joshua encouraged the children of Israel to serve God rather than what?

    a. mammon (money)
    b. principalities and powers of this dark world
    c. the gods of Egypt and of the Amorites
    d. the king of Babylon

LEG 6
ANSWERS

Jacob's

1. a. Joseph (John 4:5)
2. They had gone into the city to buy meat (John 4:8).
3. "the Jews have no dealings with the Samaritans" (John 4:9).
4. Never (John 4:14)
5. Prophet (John 4:19)
6. c. the Samaritans (John 4:40, 42)
7. c. in the mountains (John 4:20)
8. False; "ye shall neither in this mountain, nor yet at Jerusalem, worship the Father" (John 4:21).
9. Spirit, spirit (John 4:24)
10. True (John 4:25–26)
11. d. "do the will of him that sent me" (John 4:34)
12. a. asked Him that He would tarry with them (John 4:40)
13. True (John 4:42)
14. Joseph (Joshua 24:32)
15. c. the gods of Egypt and of the Amorites (Joshua 24:15)

LEG 6
WELCOME TO THE CHECK-IN MAT

Jacob's well is an interesting one because it has fresh water. Samaria was (and is) a dry country, and what little rain that does fall is caught in cisterns. Often, the standing water becomes brackish and not pleasant to drink. But a well fed from the aquifer, or underground springs, has constantly changing water. The ancients called it "living water." Water from such a source was healthy, pleasant to drink, and greatly sought after by dry, thirsty travelers.

Jesus put new meaning to the term "living water." He said, "But whosoever drinketh of the water that I shall give him shall never thirst" (John 4:14).

Did you answer 12–15 questions correctly and keep a lead in the race? Your next stop will be the hometown of the King of Kings, but a city that did not recognize His Lordship.

O Lord, the hope of Israel,
all that forsake thee shall be ashamed,
and they that depart from me shall be written in the
earth, because they have forsaken the Lord,
the fountain of living waters.
JEREMIAH 17:13

LEG 7

The race continues. Your next destination is a small town in the hill country halfway between the southern shore of the Sea of Galilee and the much larger Mediterranean Sea. The town you seek is about fifty-five miles to the northwest from Jacob's well. Because it is thirteen hundred feet above sea level, the town enjoys better weather than areas farther east and south. Breezes from the west bring moisture from the Mediterranean Sea and then release it because the air cools as it rises to the higher elevation. Check the clue box to learn where your race continues.

CLUE BOX:

Be careful when asking for directions. You can receive incomplete, misleading, or even incorrect information. To find your next location you will follow the footsteps of Jesus. He lived here for most of His life with Mary, Joseph, and His brothers and sisters (Matthew 13:55–56; Mark 6:3, Luke 4:16). Although few travelers came here in those days, an angel visited both Mary and Joseph in this town.

Race to _____.

Nazareth was in:

a. Judaea
b. Galilee

What was the name of the angel who visited Mary?

a. Gabriel
b. Michael
c. Raphael
d. The angel is not named.

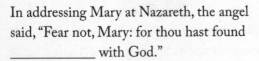

In addressing Mary at Nazareth, the angel said, "Fear not, Mary: for thou hast found _____ with God."

When she was told that she would have a child, what did Mary ask the angel?

5.

The angel told Mary that Jesus would have the throne of what Old Testament person?

a. Abraham
b. David
c. Jacob
d. Moses

6.

True or False: Mary said to the angel, "Behold the bridesmaid of the Lord."

7.

True or False: Joseph was aware that Mary was with child before the angel came to him.

8.

What name for Christ means "God with us"?

9.

When Jesus read the scripture in the synagogue at Nazareth, He:

a. sat down
b. stood up

Jesus read the passage from Esaias (Isaiah) that
says, "He hath anointed me to preach the gospel
to the _____; he hath sent me to heal
the _____, to preach deliverance to the
_____."

After reading the scripture, what did Jesus say?

    a. "A prophet is honored in his own country."
    b. "I am the one you seek."
    c. "Many are called but few are chosen."
    d. "This day is this scripture fulfilled."

Why did the people lead Jesus to the brow of the
hill on which Nazareth was built?

What did Jesus marvel at in Nazareth?

Who asked, "Can there any good thing come out of Nazareth?"

   a. Caiaphas, the chief priest
   b. Elisha, the prophet
   c. Herod, the king
   d. Nathanael, who became a disciple of Jesus

What title did Pilate put on the cross when Jesus was crucified?

LEG 7
ANSWERS

Nazareth

1. b. Galilee (Luke 1:26)
2. a. Gabriel (Luke 1:26–27)
3. Favour (Luke 1:30)
4. "How shall this be, seeing I know not a man?" (Luke 1:34)
5. b. David (Luke 1:32)
6. False; handmaid (Luke 1:38)
7. True (Matthew 1:18, 19–20)
8. Emmanuel (Matthew 1:23)
9. b. stood up (Luke 4:16)
10. Poor, brokenhearted, captives (Luke 4:18)
11. d. "This day is this scripture fulfilled" (Luke 4:21).
12. So that they might cast him down headlong (Luke 4:29)
13. Their unbelief (Mark 6:6)
14. d. Nathanael, who became a disciple of Jesus (John 1:46)
15. JESUS OF NAZARETH THE KING OF THE JEWS (John 19:19)

LEG 7
WELCOME TO THE CHECK-IN MAT

Nazareth is well known now because it was the boyhood hometown of Jesus. At the time, however, it was a little known village. Nazareth was small, with fewer than three hundred people when Joseph and Mary lived there. The fact that Mary was with child—and not yet married—could hardly go unnoticed. Yet Mary accepted her role as the handmaid of the Lord, and Joseph was an honorable man. He, too, accepted his responsibility as head of the family. He made the difficult decision to abandon his carpentry business to flee to Egypt to keep his family safe.

Your next leg of *That Amazing Place* takes you to a lake 690 feet below sea level, but unlike the Dead Sea, it is very much alive.

The spirit of the Lord God is upon me;
because the Lord hath anointed me
to preach good tidings unto the meek;
he hath sent me to bind up the brokenhearted,
to proclaim liberty to the captives,
and the opening of the prison to them that are bound.
ISAIAH 61:1

LEG 8

Your next destination is a lake, generally called a "sea" in Bible times. The lake is about thirteen miles long and eight miles wide. It is the largest freshwater lake in the region. A continuous strip of development ran around its shoreline. Along its shore were larger towns—Capernaum, Bethsaida, Tiberius and the cities of Decapolis—as well as many smaller fishing villages. The lake served as a bountiful source of fish.

Manmade breakwaters and protected harbors had been built in several places around the lake. Fishing ships and their crews needed safe places to anchor. Despite its small size, the lake could become stormy. Mountains and high land surrounded it. When cool air pushed over the mountains, it would then rush down and thrash waves on the lake's surface into sudden fury.

Clue Box:

Before being called by Jesus, four of His apostles made their living fishing in the lake. Much of Jesus' ministry occurred on its shores, and some of His miracles happened on its waters. Jesus walked on the water; He stilled a storm; and on two occasions by His command, His disciples caught a great number of fish.

Race to the Sea of _____.

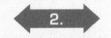

When Jesus taught the people from Simon Peter's boat on the shore of the Sea of Galilee, He:

   a.   stood up
   b.   sat down

True or False: When Jesus told His disciples to let down the net, Simon Peter explained that they had fished all night and had caught nothing.

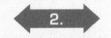

After Simon Peter asked his partners to help with the great catch of fish, what did he say to Jesus?

   a.   Behold, we will forsake all, and follow thee.
   b.   Declare unto us how this miracle is possible.
   c.   Depart from me; for I am a sinful man, O Lord.
   d.   Lord, it is good for us to be here: if thou wilt, let us learn thy ways.

In calling Simon Peter, James, and John as His disciples, what did Jesus say they would henceforth catch?

As Jesus crossed the Sea of Galilee with His disciples during a storm, and the disciples said, "Master, we perish," what was Jesus doing?

a. fishing
b. mending a net
c. praying
d. sleeping

The command Jesus gave to calm the storm was "_____, be still."

"What manner of man is this! For he commandeth even the _____ and water, and they obey him."

On the occasion when the disciples began crossing the Sea of Galilee without Jesus, what made the voyage difficult?

    a. It was night and they became lost.
    b. The people refused to let them depart.
    c. They were loaded with fish.
    d. Waves tossed the boat and the wind was contrary.

While toiling to cross the Sea of Galilee toward Capernaum without Jesus, as they saw Him walking on the water, what did the disciples say?

    a. "Be of good cheer; He will save us."
    b. "It is a sea walker."
    c. "It is a spirit."
    d. "Let us touch the hem of His garment."

Which disciple entered the water to walk to Jesus?

Jesus said to the disciple, "O thou of little
_____, wherefore didst thou doubt?"

After arriving at Capernaum and the people found
Jesus once again, why did He say they sought Him?

Jesus told those who followed Him that He was the
_____ of life.

True or False: After His resurrection, when Jesus
told Peter and the others to let down their net on
the other side of the ship, they caught so many
fish they could not be numbered.

After eating the meal by the seashore, how many
times did Jesus ask Simon Peter, "Lovest thou me?"

LEG 8
ANSWERS

Galilee

1. b. sat down (Luke 5:3)
2. True (Luke 5:5)
3. c. Depart from me; for I am a sinful man, O Lord (Luke 5:8).
4. Men (Luke 5:10)
5. d. sleeping (Luke 8:23–24)
6. Peace (Mark 4:39)
7. Winds (Luke 8:25)
8. d. Waves tossed the boat and the wind was contrary (Matthew 14:24).
9. c. "It is a spirit" (Matthew 14:26, Mark 6:49).
10. Peter (Matthew 14:29)
11. Faith (Matthew 14:31)
12. Because they'd been filled with the loaves (John 6:26)
13. Bread (John 6:35)
14. False; they caught 153 fish (John 21:11).
15. Three (John 21:15–17)

LEG 8
WELCOME TO THE CHECK-IN MAT

How did you do on this leg? Twelve to fifteen correct answers put you first at the check in. But if you came in last, take heart because you can keep on racing. The spiritual award winner is the one who keeps the faith and finishes the course. As you rest, think about the Sea of Galilee. It is 690 feet below sea level, the second lowest point on earth. Because the Jordan River flows into it and then out of it, the lake is continually refreshed. People, like lakes that give of themselves, remain fresh, alive, and vital.

Your next destination is at an important building in Jerusalem. The Bible tells us that Jesus was taken there as a baby and also as child.

They that go down to the sea in ships,
that do business in great waters;
These see the works of the Lord,
and his wonders in the deep.
For he commandeth,
and raiseth the stormy wind,
which lifteth up the waves thereof.
PSALM 107:23–25

THAT AMAZING
PLACE

LEG 9

One of the great sins a people can make is to forget what God has done for them. God allowed David to build up a great nation. But within a generation, the people chased after false gods. The central building of their worship—which is your next destination—fell into ruins.

Later it was rebuilt. But a beautiful building is not enough. Those in authority must have pure hearts. When Jesus came to Jerusalem, He was aghast at how this place of worship was mishandled by the leaders of His day. The chief priests had changed the place from a house of prayer to one in which unscrupulous businessmen cheated visitors who had come long distances to worship there.

CLUE BOX:

Jesus visited this central worship site in Jerusalem many times during His life. He was there as a baby when His parents offered a sacrifice. During the first recorded visit of His public ministry, Jesus found the place of worship falling far short of what God had intended. On His last visit, He was arrested, tried, and crucified within a week of arriving.

Race to the _____ in Jerusalem.

1.

At Jesus' presentation as a baby at the temple in Jerusalem, what sacrifice could Joseph and Mary offer according to the law of the Lord?

    a.   a lamb without spot or blemish
    b.   a pair of turtledoves or two young pigeons
    c.   burnt offerings or incense
    d.   the blood of bulls or goats

2.

Who were the two people who blessed God and gave thanks to the Lord when Jesus was presented as a baby at the temple?

    a.   Aquila and Priscilla
    b.   Nicodemus and Joanna
    c.   Simeon and Anna
    d.   Zacharias and Elisabeth

3.

Jesus would be "a light to lighten the _____, and the glory of thy people Israel."

How often did Jesus' parents go to Jerusalem?

- a.   every year at the Feast of Tabernacles
- b.   every year at the Feast of the Passover
- c.   only once at the Feast of Dedication
- d.   twice, when He was a baby and at age twelve

How many days passed before Joseph and Mary found the boy Jesus in the temple?

When His parents found Him, Jesus said, "How is it that ye sought me? wist ye not that I must be about my _____ _____? (two words)

After His public ministry began, what did Jesus do to the moneychangers in the temple?

- a.   called down fire from heaven
- b.   gave them forty stripes with a rawhide whip
- c.   overthrew their tables
- d.   struck them blind

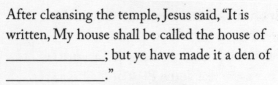

After cleansing the temple, Jesus said, "It is written, My house shall be called the house of _____; but ye have made it a den of _____."

True or False: When the Pharisees asked Jesus about paying tribute, they did so because they wanted to be taught the way of God.

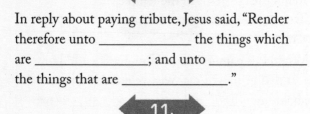

In reply about paying tribute, Jesus said, "Render therefore unto _____ the things which are _____; and unto _____ the things that are _____."

True or False: The poor woman cast in to the temple treasury one of the two mites (coins) that she possessed.

As Jesus taught in the temple and said, "There is none other commandment greater than these," what question had He answered?

What is the tenth commandment?

Why was David not allowed to build the temple?

True or False: David's son, Absalom, built the first temple.

LEG 9
ANSWERS

Temple

1. b. a pair of turtledoves or two young pigeons (Luke 2:24)
2. c. Simeon and Anna (Luke 2:25, 36)
3. Gentiles (Luke 2:32)
4. b. every year at the feast of the Passover (Luke 2:41)
5. Three (Luke 2:46)
6. Father's business (Luke 2:49)
7. c. overthrew their tables (Mark 11:15)
8. Prayer, thieves (Matthew 21:13)
9. False; they took counsel how they might entangle Him in His talk (Matthew 22:15, 17).
10. Caesar, Caesar's, God, God's (Matthew 22:21)
11. False; she gave two mites, all that she had (Mark 12:42, 44).
12. "Which is the first commandment of all?" (Mark 12:28–31).
13. Thou shalt not covet. . .any thing that is thy neighbour's (Exodus 20:17).
14. He had shed blood abundantly and made great wars (1 Chronicles 22:8).
15. False; Solomon built the temple (1 Chronicles 22:9–10).

LEG 9
WELCOME TO THE CHECK-IN MAT

King David wanted to build the temple but was told he could not do so. Instead, David made careful plans so that his son Solomon would have all he needed for it. The temple that Solomon built was a splendid building, and one of the most expensive structures ever built. The Babylonians destroyed the first temple. Later, Cyrus the Great allowed the Jews to return from Babylonian captivity. He authorized the building of another temple.

Still later, Herod the Great repaired, enlarged, and improved the second temple. His renovations were so extensive that some people called this the third temple. This is the one Jesus visited. But Jesus stated that Herod's temple would not last: "There shall not be left here one stone upon another, that shall not be thrown down" (Matthew 24:2).

Now that you have visited the temple, prepare for the dusty trip down a road that proved dangerous because thieves laid in wait for unwary travelers.

O Lord God of Israel,
there is no God like thee in the heaven,
nor in the earth; which keepest covenant,
and shewest mercy unto thy servants,
that walk before thee with all their hearts.
2 CHRONICLES 6:14

LEG 10

Your next destination is a city about seventeen miles from the temple in Jerusalem. By walking briskly, you can make the trip to the city in a day. But traveling the road alone to that city in Bible times was fraught with dangers. Most travelers did so in groups or caravans for their mutual safety.

Jesus told a parable about a certain man who fell among thieves while traveling the road to this city. It was a very true-to-life narrative to those who listened to Jesus' story. They probably had either experienced a similar event or had heard about one.

Clue Box:

In Old Testament times, strong walls protected the city. But the walls fell when Joshua's army followed God's plan for taking the city.

Race to _____.

Jesus told the story of the Good Samaritan on the road to Jericho to answer what question?

What did the thieves do to the man going down from Jerusalem to Jericho?

   a.   left him half dead
   b.   stripped him of his raiment
   c.   wounded him
   d.   all of the above

True or False: The two who passed by on the other side of the wounded man were a Pharisee and a Sadducee.

At the conclusion of the Good Samaritan parable, Jesus said to the lawyer who questioned Him, "Go, and do thou _____."

What was blind Bartimaeus doing beside the highway to Jericho?

   a. asking for prayer
   b. asking for someone to guide him because he was lost
   c. begging
   d. singing a psalm

After restoring the man's sight, Jesus said to Bartimaeus, "Go thy way; thy _____ hath made thee _____."

What was the profession of Zacchaeus?

How did Zacchaeus overcome the fact that the press of people kept him from seeing Jesus?

Jesus told Zacchaeus, "For the Son of man is come to _____ and to _____ that which was lost."

True or False: Joshua told the spies to search the country but to avoid the city of Jericho.

How did Rahab hide the two spies who entered Jericho?

    a.   at a wedding party disguised as her guests
    b.   in baskets let down from the roof
    c.   in her bedchamber
    d.   on her roof with stalks of flax

During the week before its destruction, how many times total were the priests told to go around the walls of Jericho?

    a.   six
    b.   seven
    c.   thirteen
    d.   seventy-seven

The priests were to sound horns made of the horns of what animal?

The people who went around the city with the priests were to

    a. make a continuous tumult of shouting
    b. be silent until commanded to shout

Who rescued Rahab after the walls of Jericho fell?

    a. an angel of the Lord
    b. Joshua himself
    c. the priests
    d. the two spies she had hidden

LEG 10
ANSWERS

Jericho

1. Who is my neighbour? (Luke 10:29)
2. d. all of the above (Luke 10:30)
3. False; priest and Levite (Luke 10:31–32)
4. Likewise (Luke 10:37)
5. c. begging (Mark 10:46)
6. Faith, whole (Mark 10:52)
7. Publican; tax collector (Luke 19:2)
8. He climbed up into a sycamore tree (Luke 19:4).
9. Seek, save (Luke 19:10)
10. False; view even Jericho (Joshua 2:1)
11. d. on her roof in stalks of flax (Joshua 2:6)
12. c. thirteen; six days once, seventh day seven times (Joshua 6:3–4)
13. Ram (Joshua 6:4)
14. b. be silent until commanded to shout (Joshua 6:10)
15. d. the two spies she had hidden (Joshua 6:22–23)

LEG 10
WELCOME TO THE CHECK-IN MAT

The Romans had rebuilt the road to Jericho in Jesus' day. They were the master road builders of the ancient world. In a few places, the Roman stone mileposts from that period still stand today. Although it is unlikely you could lose your way on the well-marked road, other dangers could confront you. Check your correct answers and find out how well you did in reaching the destination.

Jericho was the major city of the southern end of the Jordan Valley. The phrase "going down to Jericho" was an apt description because the road descended from 2,550 feet at Jerusalem to 820 feet below sea level near the Dead Sea. Jericho was the lowest inhabited city on earth, and a very old one, dating back to a time before Moses (Deuteronomy 34:1).

If you were the first to arrive, then tomorrow you'll be the first to take off for your next amazing place—take the road back toward Jerusalem, but stop at a small village about two miles from the larger city.

Know therefore that the Lord thy God, he is God,
the faithful God, which keepeth covenant and mercy
with them that love him and keep his commandments
to a thousand generations.
DEUTERONOMY 7:9

LEG 11

Have you been enjoying your tour of the many historic locations that Jesus visited during His ministry? All of these amazing places still exist today. Toward the close of Jesus' ministry, He came to Jerusalem for Passover week. Although He taught in the city by day, at night He retired with His followers to the Mount of Olives. On several occasions He had been well received at a small village in the same area. Read the clue box to identify this small but remarkable little village.

Clue Box:

Your destination is a small village on the Mount of Olives. Homeowners in the town prepared a meal for Jesus and His apostles. He was anointed with oil on at least two occasions. It is about two miles from Jerusalem along the road from Jerusalem to Jericho.

Race to _____.

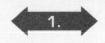

When Jesus was in Bethany in the house of Simon, how is Simon described?

    a.   Simon the lawyer
    b.   Simon the leper
    c.   Simon the Pharisee
    d.   Simon the publican

The woman who anointed Jesus in Simon's house carried the very precious ointment in what kind of box?

What type of ointment was in the box?

    a.   frankincense
    b.   myrrh
    c.   pure nard
    d.   spikenard

Jesus said, "For ye have the _____ with you always."

The woman at the house of Simon anointed Jesus on His:

a. head
b. feet

After the disciples saw the woman anoint Jesus at the house of Simon in Bethany, what did they say?

a. If this man (Jesus) were a prophet, He would know she is a sinner.
b. She did it for His burial.
c. This will be a memorial of her.
d. To what purpose is this waste?

When Jesus ate with Mary, Martha, and Lazarus, which one of the women sat at Jesus' feet?

At the home in Bethany, who received Jesus into "her" house?

a. Mary
b. Martha

Why did His disciples object to going back to Bethany when Jesus learned that Lazarus was sick?

a. It was a two-day journey.
b. Jesus had told them that Lazarus was only sleeping.
c. They could do nothing if Lazarus were dead.
d. They knew the Jewish leaders intended to stone Jesus.

Who said, "Let us also go, that we may die with him."

a. Judas who betrayed Jesus
b. Matthew, also called Levi
c. Simon, called Peter
d. Thomas, called Didymus

True or False: Martha, as soon as she heard that Jesus was coming, went and met Him, but Mary sat still in the house.

12.

True or False: Both Mary and Martha told Jesus that if He had been there their brother would not have died.

13.

True or False: Lazarus had been in the grave four days when Jesus arrived at Bethany.

14.

What command did Jesus give to bring Lazarus from the grave?

15.

After raising Lazarus from the dead, why did Jesus no longer walk openly among the Jews?

LEG 11
ANSWERS

Bethany

1. b. Simon the leper (Matthew 26:6)
2. Alabaster (Matthew 26:7)
3. d. spikenard (Mark 14:3)
4. Poor (Mark 14:7)
5. a. head (Matthew 26:7)
6. d. To what purpose is this waste? (Matthew 26:8)
7. Mary (Luke 10:39)
8. Martha (Luke 10:38)
9. d. They knew the Jewish leaders intended to stone Jesus (John 11:8).
10. d. Thomas called Didymus (John 11:16)
11. True (John 11:20)
12. True (John 11:21, 32)
13. True (John 11:39)
14. Lazarus, come forth (John 11:43).
15. The chief priests and the Pharisees sought to put Him to death (John 11:47, 53–54).

Thou preparest a table before me in the presence of mine enemies: thou anointest my head with oil; my cup runneth over.
PSALM 23:5

LEG 11
WELCOME TO THE CHECK-IN MAT

The Bible story of Lazarus reveals a distinctive difference in the personalities of Martha and Mary. Mary, on the first two occasions that she is mentioned in the Bible, is sitting. She sat at Jesus' feet to hear His words (Luke 10:39). She sat still in the house while her sister ran to meet Jesus after the death of Lazarus (John 11:20).

On the other hand, Martha is portrayed as a hard-working person. Apparently, Martha not only prepared the food for Jesus and His followers, but she also served them single-handedly. (The Bible makes no mention of servants.) The guest list probably included well over a dozen people: Jesus, twelve apostles, perhaps others, in addition to Martha herself, Lazarus, and Mary. As host of such a large number, Martha must have been exceptionally industrious.

Despite their differences, the Bible says Jesus loved them both (John 11:5). The story of Martha, Mary, and Lazarus is a gentle reminder that His love reaches out to encourage all people to welcome Him into their lives.

Your next destination is nearby. In fact, merely step outside Martha's house in Bethany, stroll a few feet to an olive grove, and you will be there.

LEG 12

After a time of rest and reflection, walk now to a garden near the foot of the western slope of the mount on which Bethany is located. It is right across the Kidron Valley from Jerusalem. The name of the garden means "oil press," a reference to an olive oil press that must have been located on the hillside at one time. Check the clue box for additional details.

Clue Box:

Your destination is an olive grove on a hillside. It is a small ridge-like mountain east of Jerusalem where Jesus came for private instruction of His apostles. He prayed in the garden on its slopes before He was betrayed and arrested. Forty days later, it was on this same mountainside that His apostles watched as He was received into heaven.

Walk to the Garden of _____ on the Mount of _____.

True or False: Every morning people came from the temple to the Mount of Olives to be taught by Jesus.

How many disciples did Jesus send to bring the colt (young donkey) to Him?

If anyone asked why they took the colt, what did Jesus tell His disciples to do?

a. Pay for the colt with a wineskin full of new wine.
b. Say, "He was born for this day."
c. Say, "The colt shall go where he wilt."
d. Say, "The Lord hath need of him."

Jesus' disciples asked, "What shall be the sign of thy coming, and of the end of the _____?"

As Jesus entered the city riding on the colt, what did the people do?

   a. called insults to Him
   b. hurled stones at Him
   c. spread flax and flower petals on the way
   d. spread garments and tree branches on the way

True or False: Although many would come in the name of Christ, they would be unable to deceive anyone.

On the night of His betrayal, immediately before they left the upper room for the Mount of Olives, what did Jesus and His disciples do?

   a. kneelt in prayer
   b. lit torches because the night was dark
   c. read from the prophet Esaias (Isaiah)
   d. sang a song

Peter said, "Though I should die with thee, yet will I not _____ thee."

What were the names of the three apostles that Jesus took a little farther with Him in the Garden of Gethsemane as He prayed?

What did the three apostles do as Jesus prayed?

    a. kept watch
    b. prayed
    c. sang
    d. slept

"The _____ indeed is willing, but the _____ is weak."

True or False: While He was in the garden, an angel came to Jesus from heaven and strengthened Him.

To what does the Gospel of Luke compare the sweat of Jesus?

Which ear of Malchus, the high priest's servant, did Peter cut off?

As He ascended, where did Jesus tell His apostles to tarry for the power from on high?

a. Bethany
b. Bethlehem
c. Galilee
d. Jerusalem

LEG 12
ANSWERS

Gethsemane, Olives

1. False; He taught at the temple (John 8:1–2).
2. Two (Luke 19:29–30)
3. d. Say, "The Lord hath need of him" (Luke 19:34).
4. World (Matthew 24:3)
5. d. spread garments and tree branches on the way (Mark 11:8)
6. False; they would deceive many (Matthew 24:5).
7. d. sang a song (Mark 14:26)
8. Deny (Matthew 26:35)
9. Peter, James, John (Mark 14:33)
10. d. slept (Mark 14:37, 40)
11. Spirit, flesh (Matthew 26:41)
12. True (Luke 22:43)
13. Great drops of blood (Luke 22:44)
14. Right (John 18:10)
15. d. Jerusalem (Luke 24:49)

LEG 12
WELCOME TO THE CHECK-IN MAT

How did you do in answering the questions? Perhaps you found some of them difficult. Certainly the events of that night in the garden must have been confusing and difficult for Jesus' apostles to understand. They found the next three days to be bewildering and frightening, too. But Jesus' crucifixion was not the end of the story. He arose, and during the next forty days He gave final instructions to His followers (Acts 1:3).

During the time of Jesus, the Mount of Olives was outwardly a pleasant and restful place. But it had been associated with a betrayal once before. In the Old Testament, David fled there barefoot and weeping after being betrayed by his son, Absalom (2 Samuel 15:30–31). Today, a few ancient olive trees are left, but most of the hillside has become a cemetery.

Your next destination is not only a small village, but also the road that takes you there.

I will ransom them
from the power of the grave;
I will redeem them from death:
O death, I will be thy plagues;
O grave, I will be thy destruction:
repentance shall be hid from mine eyes.
HOSEA 13:14

THAT AMAZING
PLACE

LEG 13

This amazing place is a road where Jesus walked and talked with two disciples on the road to their village. It was shortly after His resurrection. According to the Gospel of Luke, the distance from Jerusalem to the village was about seven or eight miles. The walk would probably have taken a little over two hours, perhaps longer if they slowed as they talked.

CLUE BOX:

Walk from the Mount of Olives to Jerusalem. Your goal from there is both a road and a village on the road. Two disciples walked home along this road on Sunday, the day of the Lord's resurrection. He drew near and walked with them, but they did not recognize Him. In a brief but accurate account, they summarize the events leading to the death of Jesus of Nazareth.

Walk along the road to _____.

How did Jesus describe the emotions of the two disciples on the road to Emmaus?

   a. angry
   b. contrite
   c. happy
   d. sad

Of the two disciples on the road to Emmaus, what was the name of the disciple who answered Jesus when He asked, "What manner of communications are there that ye have one to another?"

   a. Cleopas
   b. Gaius
   c. Sopater
   d. Timothy

The first ones to the empty tomb of Jesus were:

   a. men
   b. women

Who was the first apostle to enter the empty tomb of Jesus?

Jesus began with which prophet in explaining what the prophets said about Himself?

In speaking of the Passover Lamb, Moses instructed them to:

    a.   break every bone of it
    b.   not break any bone of it

What Old Testament writer does Peter quote in Acts: "A prophet shall the Lord your God raise up unto you of your brethren, like unto me"?

    a.   Ezekiel
    b.   Jeremiah
    c.   Micah
    d.   Moses

In Acts 13:35, Paul quotes a psalm in which God says He will not allow His Holy One to see what?

In Romans, Paul quotes Esaias (Isaiah): "There shall be a root of Jesse, and he that shall rise to reign over the _____; in him shall the _____ trust" (same word).

What does Isaiah say will be swallowed up in victory?

Isaiah writes, "I lay in Zion for a foundation a _____, a tried _____, a precious corner _____, a sure foundation" (same word).

True or False: The two disciples returned to Jerusalem to tell the eleven that they had seen Jesus alive.

13.

Who in the Old Testament had a night vision similar to the one John describes in Revelation: "And I looked, and behold a white cloud, and upon the cloud one sat like unto the Son of man."

   a. Daniel
   b. Haggai
   c. Jonah
   d. Solomon

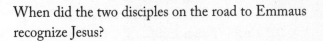

14.

When did the two disciples on the road to Emmaus recognize Jesus?

   a. when He first began walking with them
   b. when He described how the prophets spoke of Him
   c. when He took bread and blessed it
   d. when they returned to Jerusalem and saw Him the second time

15.

True or False: When Jesus and the two disciples arrived at the village, He said, "Let us abide here together."

LEG 13
ANSWERS

Emmaus

1. d. sad (Luke 24:17)
2. a. Cleopas (Luke 24:18)
3. b. women (Luke 24:22)
4. Simon Peter (John 20:5–6)
5. Moses (Luke 24:27)
6. b. not break any bone of it (Numbers 9:12)
7. d. Moses (Acts 3:22, Deuteronomy 18:18)
8. Corruption (Acts 13:35, Psalm 16:10)
9. Gentiles (Romans 15:12, Isaiah 11:10)
10. Death (Isaiah 25:8)
11. Stone (Isaiah 28:16)
12. True (Luke 24:33, 34)
13. a. Daniel (Daniel 7:13, Revelation 14:14)
14. c. when He took bread and blessed it (Luke 24:30–31)
15. False: they said, "Abide with us" (Luke 24:29).

LEG 13
WELCOME TO THE CHECK-IN MAT

This was one of the harder legs, not because of the distance, but because the questions ranged throughout the Old Testament concerning what the prophets said about Jesus. If you managed to answer at least twelve correct, consider yourself fortunate and experienced in making the trek through the Bible.

The two disciples were sad when Jesus met them because they could not fathom the reason for the death of a mighty prophet. Jesus gave the reason. Beginning with Moses, He explained that the Savior would suffer the indignities of the crucifixion. Jesus asked, "Ought not Christ to have suffered these things, and to enter into his glory?" (Luke 24:26).

The two disciples showed their hospitality to a stranger by asking Jesus to stay with them rather than continuing on after nightfall. Once He revealed Himself and then vanished, they could not wait until morning to share the news. They immediately—at night—walked back to Jerusalem to tell the eleven apostles and other believers that Jesus had risen.

Why do the heathen rage, and the people imagine a vain thing? The kings of the earth set themselves, and the rulers take counsel together, against the Lord, and against his anointed.

PSALM 2:1–2

LEG 14

Life, in the spiritual sense, can be as challenging as any physical effort. During the forty days from the time of His resurrection to His ascension, one of Jesus' most frequent statements to His apostles and disciples was, "Fear not." At the time of His arrest, their courage had vanished. Sometimes we can be dejected, too.

But after His apostles saw the risen Christ, something happened. They received strength from the Comforter whom Jesus had promised to send after His ascension (John 16:7). Soon, the apostles were put to the test before the powerful religious council in Jerusalem. Their unwavering determination to speak the truth became a powerful example to others who served the Lord.

Clue Box:

The encounter of Peter and John with the priests and the Sadducees begins with a notable miracle of the healing of a lame man. Peter and John are put in prison overnight, called before the council the next day, and then threatened. What would happen? Continue to your next amazing place by finding where it all began when a lame man sat at a gate to the temple.

Return to Jerusalem to the gate called _____.

How long had the man at the gate called "Beautiful" been lame?

The lame man was taken to the gate called "Beautiful" for what purpose?

    a.   to ask for alms
    b.   to be examined by a priest
    c.   to be healed by having the shadow of the apostles fall upon him
    d.   to praise God and see the salvation of Jesus

Peter told the lame man, "_____ and _____ have I none; but such as I have give I thee."

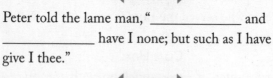

True or False: Peter took the lame man by his right hand and lifted him up.

5.

After his feet and anklebones received strength, what did the lame man do?

    a.   began walking
    b.   began leaping
    c.   began praising God
    d.   all of the above

6.

True or False: After his healing, the lame man immediately left the temple area and returned home to show himself to his parents, friends, and neighbors.

7.

The people came to what place in the temple area to ask Peter and John about the miracle?

    a.   Pool of Bethesda
    b.   Pool of Siloam
    c.   Sheep gate
    d.   Solomon's Porch

"Why look ye so earnestly on us, as though by our own _____ or holiness we had made this man to walk?"

Peter said the men of Israel denied Jesus in the presence of what person who was determined to let Him go?

One of those who arrested Peter and John was:

a. a Roman centurion
b. the captain of the temple

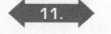

What did Peter and the apostles preach that grieved the priests and Sadducees?

a. God sent Jesus to curse unbelievers.
b. Only the poor could be saved.
c. That miracles brought glory to believers of Christ.
d. Through Jesus was the resurrection of the dead.

When the council asked by what power or by what name Peter had done the healing miracle, what answer did Peter give?

"For there is none other name under heaven given among men, whereby we must be _____."

True or False: The council decided to deny that a notable miracle had been done.

Peter asked the council whether it would be better to hearken to them or to whom?

LEG 14
ANSWERS

Beautiful

1. Since birth, above forty years (Acts 3:2, 4:22)
2. a. to ask for alms (Acts 3:2)
3. Silver, gold (Acts 3:6)
4. True (Acts 3:7)
5. d. all of the above (Acts 3:8)
6. False; he entered the temple with Peter and John (Acts 3:8).
7. d. Solomon's Porch (Acts 3:11)
8. Power (Acts 3:12)
9. Pilate (Acts 3:13)
10. b. the captain of the temple (Acts 4:1, 3)
11. d. Through Jesus was the resurrection from the dead (Acts 4:2).
12. By the name of Jesus Christ of Nazareth (Acts 4:10)
13. Saved (Acts 4:12)
14. False; they could not deny it (Acts 4:16).
15. God (Acts 4:19)

LEG 14
WELCOME TO THE CHECK-IN MAT

Like Peter and John, sometimes we must choose between truth and lies and between courage and flight. Peter's statement, "Whether it be right in the sight of God to hearken unto you more than unto God, judge ye," ranks with that of Joshua's words, "But as for me and my house, we will serve the LORD" (Joshua 24:15). Peter's cool confidence strengthens any of us who must face similar hostile encounters with unbelievers.

Jesus had commanded the apostles to wait in Jerusalem for the "power from on high" (Luke 24:49). But He also told them to "Go ye therefore, and teach all nations" (Matthew 28:19). As the believers were strengthening in Jerusalem, their numbers multiplied. They began implementing the second command. They expanded both ethnically and geographically. After a mandatory rest stop, your next leg will follow Philip as he travels beyond the borders of Judea.

And it shall come to pass in the last days,
that the mountain of the Lord's house shall be
established in the top of the mountains,
and shall be exalted above the hills;
and all nations shall flow unto it.
ISAIAH 2:2

THAT AMAZING
PLACE

LEG 15

When you travel, do you enjoy city tours, or do you prefer visits into the countryside? The next amazing place takes you away from the heavily populated Jerusalem. It is also an excursion into a region that most Jews avoided. In fact, from now on, your travels will take you farther and farther from the center of Judaism.

Following the courageous actions of Peter and John, the number of believers increased. The apostles appointed seven servants to see that all those in need received proper care. One of the seven Grecian servants, Stephen, became the first Christian to die for the new faith.

Philip, a coworker of Stephen, eventually left Jerusalem. He traveled north to a city in a province with the same name between Judaea and Galilee.

CLUE BOX:

Philip was well received despite initial opposition by a magician named Simon. When reports of Philip's work reached the disciples in Jerusalem, they sent two apostles to check it out. Your next destination is the city where Simon the Sorcerer lived. In the Old Testament, it was the home of King Ahab.

Go to _____.

Why did Christians leave Jerusalem and enter Samaria?

   a. because of a famine in Judaea
   b. because of persecution
   c. Samaritan believers asked them to come.
   d. They could no longer worship at the
       temple.

Who was the person that consented to the death of Stephen and made havoc of the church?

True or False: The persecution caused the apostles to be "scattered abroad."

True or False: Philip was mighty in word, but could not do any miracles.

Which phrase describes how the people of Samaria received Philip's preaching?

    a.   listened but turned away the truth
    b.   refused to listen
    c.   were greatly troubled
    d.   gave heed with great joy

True or False: Simon the sorcerer believed and was baptized.

When the apostles heard that the Samaritans had received the word, whom did they send to pray for them?

What power did Simon the sorcerer wish to buy from the apostles?

"Thy money perish with thee, because thou hast thought that the _____ of God may be purchased with money."

"Thou hast neither part nor lot in this matter: for thy _____ is not right in the sight of God."

What was Simon the Sorcerer's reaction when told that he was in the gall of bitterness and in the bond of iniquity?

    a. He asked for prayer.
    b. He became the chief spokesman against Philip and the apostles.
    c. He died unrepentant.
    d. He shook dust from his feet and left Samaria.

What was the name of Ahab's wife who schemed to kill Naboth?

In the Old Testament, what did Ahab, King of Samaria, try to buy from Naboth the Jezreelite?

   a. a coat of many colors
   b. a golden calf
   c. a vineyard
   d. a pure white, wild stallion on which no one had ridden

"Thus saith the LORD, In the place where dogs licked the _____ of Naboth shall dogs lick thy _____." (same word)

True or False: Following the word from the Lord, Ahab humbled himself and God delayed the punishment.

LEG 15
ANSWERS

Samaria

1. b. because of persecution (Acts 8:1)
2. Saul (Paul) (Acts 7:59, 8:1, 3)
3. False; believers were scattered, except the apostles (Acts 8:1).
4. False; he did do miracles (Acts 8:6–7).
5. d. gave heed with great joy (Acts 8:6, 8)
6. True (Acts 8:9, 13)
7. Peter and John (Acts 8:14)
8. The power to lay on hands to give others the Holy Ghost (Acts 8:19)
9. Gift (Acts 8:20)
10. Heart (Acts 8:21)
11. a. He asked for prayer (Acts 8:24).
12. Jezebel (1 Kings 21:7)
13. c. a vineyard (1 Kings 21:1–2)
14. Blood (1 Kings 21:19)
15. True (1 Kings 21:29)

LEG 15
WELCOME TO THE CHECK-IN MAT

How many questions did you answer? Were you the first to arrive with twelve or more questions correct, or the last to arrive with three or fewer correct? The race is not always to the swift. You must pay attention to the route markers—the Bible—to ensure you are not running around and accomplishing nothing.

This leg was set in Samaria. Because of events that happened centuries before, Jews considered the Samaritans heretics and would not associate with them. But after Philip's successful missionary work in Samaria, Peter and John accepted the Samaritans and ensured that Christianity would continue to expand until the Gospel was, indeed, taken to all nations.

After a rest, it is time to head on to the next amazing place. You will follow Philip into southern Palestine near the border with Egypt.

And in very deed for this cause have I raised thee up,
for to show in thee my power; and that
my name may be declared
throughout all the earth.
EXODUS 9:16

THAT AMAZING
PLACE

LEG 16

Philip was one of the seven men the apostles had chosen to remedy the Grecian widows being overlooked in the distribution of food in Jerusalem. Philip later settled in Caesarea where he met with Paul, the very man who had consented to the death of Stephen, another of the seven servants.

When Philip's work in Samaria was finished, he was given another traveling assignment. His destination was in the region where Samson toppled the Temple of Dagon on his enemies, losing his life in the process.

CLUE BOX:

Travel to what was once part of the land of the Philistines. It is located south of Judaea but northeast of Egypt. Samson's Philistine enemies incorrectly thought they had him trapped in a city of this land. In this same area, Philip explained a passage of Old Testament scripture to a man traveling in a chariot.

Race to the next amazing place: _____.

Why did Philip go unto Gaza?

    a.   An angel told him to.
    b.   His four daughters lived there.
    c.   He accompanied Peter who went there.
    d.   The Jerusalem elders sent him there.

How does the book of Acts describe Gaza?

    a.   as a desert
    b.   as hill country
    c.   as the Plain of Gaza
    d.   as the Wilderness of Gaza

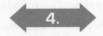

Who was Candace?

What was the man of Ethiopia's profession?

    a.   a scribe
    b.   the chief of palace guards
    c.   the chief of stables
    d.   the queen's treasurer

Why had the Ethiopian eunuch gone to Jerusalem?

What prophet was the Ethiopian eunuch reading?

True or False: The eunuch understood what he read.

The scripture read, "He was led as a _____
to the slaughter."

True or False: Philip used the very scripture the
Eunuch read to preach Jesus to him.

When Philip told the eunuch he could be baptized
if he believed, how did the eunuch reply?

    a. "I believe in the King of Israel."
    b. "I believe that Jesus Christ is the Son of
        God."
    c. "I believe; help mine unbelief."
    d. "I do believe and tremble."

The book of Acts says that the eunuch went on his way:

    a. greatly troubled
    b. rejoicing

How is Samson described in the twenty years after he killed one thousand Philistines?

    a. judge
    b. king
    c. prophet
    d. warrior

When trapped in the city of Gaza, what display of strength did Samson do to escape the city?

What woman conspired with the Philistines to learn the strength of Samson?

After having his hair cut and being blinded, what labor—normally done by animals—did his captors have Samson do in the Gaza prison house?

LEG 16
ANSWERS

Gaza

1. a. An angel told him to (Acts 8:26).
2. a. as a desert (Acts 8:26)
3. Queen of the Ethiopians (Acts 8:27)
4. d. the queen's treasurer (Acts 8:27)
5. To worship (Acts 8:27)
6. Esaias (Isaiah) (Acts 8:28)
7. False; he needed guidance (Acts 8:30–31).
8. Sheep (Acts 8:32)
9. True (Acts 8:35)
10. b. "I believe that Jesus Christ is the Son of God" (Acts 8:37).
11. b. rejoicing (Acts 8:39)
12. a. judge (Judges 15:16, 20)
13. He tore off the doors of the city gate and carried them away (Judges 16:3).
14. Delilah (Judges 16:4–5)
15. Grind (grain) (Judges 16:21)

LEG 16
WELCOME TO THE CHECK-IN MAT

Congratulations! You've finished more than half of the race. Your travels to Bible places have been challenging—but not so difficult as to be impossible to finish. At times, serving God can be challenging, too. But He will never send us a task that we are unable to complete.

When Philip was sent into Gaza, he must have wondered what purpose that would serve. It was a desert place, thinly populated, and must have seemed a poor location to preach Jesus. But if the eunuch was the only convert that Philip made there, it served an important purpose. The eunuch was a dedicated individual who traveled from Ethiopia to worship in Jerusalem. He would have been a talented person to rise to chief of the Queen of Ethiopia's treasury. His conversion must have fueled further successes in Africa.

Once you have rested, your next amazing place is a city where another person, a prophet of God, also raced. But he was running from the call of God.

He was oppressed, and he was afflicted,
yet he opened not his mouth: he is brought as a lamb
to the slaughter, and as a sheep before her shearers is
dumb, so he openeth not his mouth.
Isaiah 53:7

THAT AMAZING
PLACE

LEG 17

It is time to set out again. Head north up the Mediterranean coast from Gaza to one of the oldest and most important harbors of ancient times. The harbor had a reef that served as a breakwater with a natural entrance on the north side. Large ships could drop anchor in the protected water, while smaller vessels could be pulled up on the sandy beach.

CLUE BOX:

The next amazing place is forty miles west of Jerusalem and the closest harbor to that city on the Mediterranean Sea. The cedars of Lebanon for building and then rebuilding the temple were shipped ashore at this seaside town (2 Chronicles 2:16 and Ezra 3:7). Peter traveled to the city to raise a beloved Christian woman from the dead. Later, while Peter prayed, God gave him a vision to announce that Gentile believers would be accepted into Christian fellowship.

Race to _____.

Tabitha, the woman in Joppa who became sick and died, was also known by what other name?

a. Dorcas
b. Lydia
c. Sophia
d. Urbana

True or False: Peter was in Joppa when Tabitha's friends sent for him.

What did Tabitha's friends show Peter when he came to the upper chamber where they had laid her?

Cornelius was a centurion of the band called the _____ band.

How is Cornelius described?

   a.   as a devout man
   b.   as a fierce warrior
   c.   as a learned scholar
   d.   as a secret Christian

The Lord told Cornelius, "Thy prayers and thine
_____ are come up for a memorial before
God."

What was the profession of Simon of Joppa?

True or False: Cornelius went to Joppa to see Peter.

Peter was in what city when he fell into a trance and saw the vision of animals let down from heaven?

    a.   Caesarea
    b.   Jerusalem
    c.   Joppa
    d.   Lydda

Why had Peter gone to the housetop?

What did God tell Peter to do with the animals he saw in the trance?

    a.   clean them
    b.   free them
    c.   kill and eat
    d.   sacrifice them

What type of animal was NOT specifically listed as being in the sheet of the vision?

    a.   creeping things
    b.   four-footed beasts
    c.   fowls of the air
    d.   sheep

"Not so, Lord; for I have never eaten any thing that is _____ or _____."

How many times did the trance repeat itself?

True or False: Peter immediately understood the vision he had seen.

LEG 17
ANSWERS

Joppa

1. a. Dorcas (Acts 9:36)
2. False; in Lydda (Acts 9:38)
3. Coats and garments she had made (Acts 9:39)
4. Italian (Acts 10:1)
5. a. as a devout man (Acts 10:2)
6. Alms (Acts 10:4)
7. Tanner (Acts 10:6)
8. False; he sent two servants and a devout soldier (Acts 10:7–8).
9. c. Joppa (Acts 9:43, 10:11–12)
10. To pray (Acts 10:9)
11. c. kill and eat (Acts 10:13)
12. d. sheep (Acts 10:12)
13. Common, unclean (Acts 10:14)
14. Thrice (three times) (Acts 10:16)
15. False; he doubted what it meant (Acts 10:17).

LEG 17
WELCOME TO THE CHECK-IN MAT

Joppa is an ancient city. It is mentioned several places in the Bible, beginning with the division of the Promised Land among the twelve tribes (Joshua 19:46, called "Japho" in that passage). The city became a jumping-off place for sea travelers. Jonah left from Joppa on his vain voyage to avoid carrying God's message to the people of Nineveh.

Like Jonah, Peter did not immediately embrace God's command. When God told him to kill and eat the unclean animals, Peter made one of the most infamous remarks of his life—saying "Not so" to God and calling Him "Lord" in the same short sentence (Acts 10:14).

Sometimes we come face to face with a clear command of God. Perhaps we say "not so," as well. But as God instructs us, guides us, and strengthens us, the "not so" becomes "yes, I will."

Enjoy your seaside visit and prepare for your race to the next amazing place—a Roman city—as evidenced by its very name being based on the title of Roman rulers.

I will also give thee for a light to the Gentiles,
that thou mayest be my salvation
unto the end of the earth.
ISAIAH 49:6

THAT AMAZING
PLACE

LEG 18

Get ready. Your mandatory rest period is nearly over. For your next destination, follow Peter from Joppa as he travels thirty miles to the north to a Roman city. Today, the city is in ruins. And for a generation before the time of Peter it was in ruins, as well. But Herod the Great rebuilt it with an artificial harbor, theater, and race course. A Roman army officer named Cornelius was stationed there.

About ten years had passed since the apostles delivered the first sermon on the day of Pentecost. During that time the Gospel had been preached only to traditional Jews, those who converted to Judaism, and Samaritans. Many believers thought a person could not become a Christian without first becoming a Jew. But the conversion of Cornelius proved otherwise.

CLUE BOX:

Go to the city where Cornelius the centurion had a vision and called for Peter. The events that took place in the city where he lived showed that nothing prevented believing Gentiles, such as Cornelius, from accepting Christ. Years later, the apostle Paul would face trials in the same city.

The next amazing place is _____.

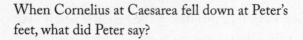

When Cornelius at Caesarea fell down at Peter's feet, what did Peter say?

    a. "God to the Gentiles hath granted repentance unto life."
    b. "I am anointed to be a judge of the quick and the dead."
    c. "No man must be called unclean."
    d. "Stand up; I myself also am a man."

2.

True or False: The man in white clothing who told Cornelius to send for Peter was NOT an angel.

3.

"Of a truth I perceive that God is no _____ of persons."

4.

What fell upon Cornelius and the others that caused Peter to say, "Can any man forbid water, that these should not be baptized?"

When the circumcised believers heard Peter's explanation as to why he baptized Cornelius they:

    a. became angry
    b. glorified God

Who said, "Why tempt ye God, to put a yoke upon the neck of the disciples, which neither our fathers nor we were able to bear?"

Who was the believer who lived in Caesarea and had four unmarried daughters that prophesized?

    a. Anaias
    b. Claudius Lysias
    c. Gamaliel
    d. Philip the evangelist

When Agabus bound his hands and feet with Paul's girdle, what event did that signify?

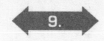

True or False: After his arrest, Paul was taken from Jerusalem to Caesarea in daylight by a small band of about a dozen soldiers.

What was the name of Felix's Jewish wife?

a. Bernice
b. Claudia
c. Drusilla
d. Porcius

"Go thy way for this time; when I have a _____ season, I will call for thee."

Who was the Caesar in Rome at the time of Paul's trial before Festus?

a. Augustus
b. Claudius
c. Nero
d. The Bible does not identify him.

Touching his religion, Paul said that from his youth he had lived as a strict _____.

Who said, "Almost thou persuadest me to be a Christian"?

Agrippa said that Paul would have been released if he hadn't done what?

   a.   appealed to Caesar
   b.   defiled the temple
   c.   offended the Jews
   d.   said that Jesus of Nazareth was a king

LEG 18
ANSWERS

Caesarea

1. d. "Stand up; I myself also am a man" (Acts 10:26).
2. False; Peter describes him as an angel (Acts 10:31–32; Acts 11:13).
3. Respecter (Acts 10:34)
4. The Holy Ghost (Acts 10:47)
5. b. glorified God (Acts 11:1–2, 18)
6. Peter (Acts 15:7, 10)
7. d. Philip the evangelist (Acts 21:8–9)
8. How Paul would be bound in Jerusalem (Acts 21:11)
9. False; at night by two centurions and 470 military men (Acts 23:23, 31)
10. c. Drusilla (Acts 24:24)
11. Convenient (Acts 24:25)
12. a. Augustus (Acts 25:21)
13. Pharisee (Acts 26:5)
14. Agrippa (Acts 26:28)
15. a. appealed to Caesar (Acts 26:32)

LEG 18
WELCOME TO THE CHECK-IN MAT

How well did you fare on this leg? Mark yourself excellent if you missed only two or three questions. Doing so well shows real knowledge about Caesarea and the events that occurred there.

From the beginning, God had planned for Jesus to be the Savior of the world; of both Jews and Gentiles. Peter traveled to Caesarea and preached to Cornelius, explaining that any person who obeys God's will is acceptable to Him. Cornelius was baptized without first becoming a Jew. The acceptance of Gentiles into Christianity had a profound impact on the growth of the church.

After a time to rest, your next destination is the place where God called the apostle who would earn the title "apostle to the Gentiles."

After those days, saith the Lord,
I will put my law in their inward parts,
and write it in their hearts; and will be their God,
and they shall be my people.
JEREMIAH 31:33

LEG 19

The challenge of finding your next amazing place will begin shortly. Your destination became a stronghold of Christianity. At first, persecution of Christians had been confined to the region around Judaea. But as Christianity grew and spread, so did the opposition. The leading adversary was Saul (later called "Paul"). His efforts to stamp out the new faith caused believers to scatter even farther. Some traveled nearly 170 miles north to a town in Syria.

Clue Box:

You will travel to a city where Saul planned to take Christians captive and bring them back to Jerusalem for trial. On the road to that city, however, something happened that changed Saul from the chief opponent of Christianity to its most vocal supporter.

Travel to the city of _____.

True or False: In Damascus, Saul (Paul) intended to arrest both men and women.

"Saul, Saul, why _____ thou me?"

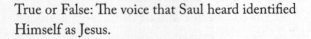

True or False: The voice that Saul heard identified Himself as Jesus.

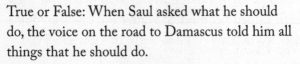

True or False: When Saul asked what he should do, the voice on the road to Damascus told him all things that he should do.

How many days was Saul blind?

Paul was in Damascus on a street called:

a. Narrow
b. Straight

In whose house did Paul stay while in Damascus?

   a. Ananias
   b. Barnabas
   c. Judas
   d. Simon

Saul was chosen by Jesus to carry His name "before the _____, and kings, and the children of Israel."

Who was the first person to address Saul as "Brother Saul"?

   a. Ananias
   b. Barnabas
   c. John
   d. Peter

10.

"And now why tarriest thou? arise, and be _____, and _____ away thy sins, calling on the name of the Lord."

11.

After the Jews sought to kill Saul for preaching Christ in the synagogues, how did Saul escape from Damascus?

    a. by being raised from the dead after being stoned and carried from the city
    b. by an escort of Roman soldiers
    c. by being let down the city wall in a basket by the disciples
    d. by being carried away in a wagon load of flax

12.

Who was the disciple who introduced Saul to the apostles in Jerusalem?

Who was Gamaliel?

In what city had Saul been born?

When telling Agrippa of the events on the road to Damascus, how did Paul describe the light that shown around him?

a. above the brightness of the sun
b. as a bleached sheet
c. as shining as gold
d. more blinding than lightning

LEG 19
ANSWERS

Damascus

1. True (Acts 9:2)
2. Persecutest (Acts 9:4)
3. True (Acts 9:5)
4. False; Saul would be told what to do in Damascus (Acts 9:6; 22:10).
5. Three (Acts 9:9)
6. b. Straight (Acts 9:11)
7. c. Judas (Acts 9:11)
8. Gentiles (Acts 9:15)
9. a. Ananias (Acts 9:17)
10. Baptized, wash (Acts 22:16)
11. c. by being let down the city wall in a basket by the disciples (Acts 9:25)
12. Barnabas (Acts 9:27)
13. The one who taught Saul in Jerusalem (Acts 22:3)
14. Tarsus (Acts 22:3)
15. a. above the brightness of the sun (Acts 26:13)

LEG 19
WELCOME TO THE CHECK-IN MAT

Check your score for this leg. Did you race in first, stay with the rest in the middle, or struggle to finish? Regardless of your current standing, each leg provides an opportunity to improve your results. Accept the challenge and keep on racing.

In Acts 8, the Bible introduced Paul (Saul) as a violent enemy of Christianity. The book of Acts ends with Paul as its most capable defender. How that change came about is described in Acts 9. Jesus did not tell Paul all that he should do. Instead, He gave that assignment to Ananias. Paul learned that human action is the primary means of spreading the Gospel.

After his conversion, Paul upheld the Christian faith as fervently as he'd opposed it earlier. He became the subject of persecution rather than the instigator of it. He also traveled extensively and preached in some of the chief cities of Asia and Europe. Your next amazing place is a city in Turkey that had become the eastern headquarters of the Roman Empire.

We are troubled on every side, yet not distressed;
we are perplexed, but not in despair;
Persecuted, but not forsaken;
cast down, but not destroyed.

2 CORINTHIANS 4:8–9

THAT AMAZING
PLACE

LEG 20

With the acceptance of Gentiles into the fellowship of disciples, the apostles in Jerusalem learned of an explosive growth of the church in a city far from Jerusalem. The city was about two hundred miles north of Damascus in northern Syria. (It is now located in southern Turkey because of a change in international borders.) The city was the third most important city in the Roman Empire, surpassed only by Alexandria in Egypt and Rome itself. Among its half of a million inhabitants was a growing number of Gentile Christians.

CLUE BOX:

The apostles in Jerusalem sent Barnabas to review the situation in this important city. He, in turn, found Paul and together they preached in the city. In this city, disciples of Jesus were called by a new name for the first time.

Your next amazing place is _____.

The first group of disciples left Jerusalem for
Antioch following the death of which individual?

a. an unnamed Gentile believer
b. James the apostle
c. Jesus
d. Stephen

What caused the church in Jerusalem to send
Barnabas to Antioch?

When Barnabas came to Antioch he was:

a. dismayed
b. glad at what he saw

After visiting the Antioch church, to what city did
Barnabas travel to find Saul (Paul)?

The disciples were called _____ first in Antioch.

What prophet came from Jerusalem to Antioch and predicted a dearth (famine) that came about during the reign of Claudius Caesar?

a. Agabus
b. Judas
c. Lucius of Cyrene
d. Simon, also known as Niger

True or False: The believers in Judaea sent famine relief to those in Antioch.

Who decided that Barnabas and Saul should leave Antioch on a missionary journey?

a. Barnabas and Saul themselves
b. the elders at Antioch
c. the elders at Jerusalem
d. the Holy Ghost

9.

When Barnabas and Saul began their missionary journey, they took with them _____, whose surname was _____.

10.

The meeting that convened to consider the question of whether Gentile believers must keep the Law of Moses was held in the city of _____.

11.

True or False: The Jews had been unable to keep the Law of Moses.

12.

Who said, "My sentence is, that we trouble not them, which from among the Gentiles are turned to God"?

   a. Barnabas
   b. James
   c. Paul
   d. Peter

The Gentile believers were to abstain from pollution of idols, from fornication, from things strangled, and from what else?

True or False: Except for Paul, no other apostle ever visited Antioch.

True or False: Paul returned to Antioch time and again because he was never persecuted in that city.

LEG 20
ANSWERS

Antioch

1. d. Stephen (Acts 11:19)
2. They had heard a large number of Grecians (Gentiles) had become believers (Acts 11:20–22).
3. b. glad at what he saw (Acts 11:22–23)
4. Tarsus (Acts 11:25)
5. Christians (Acts 11:26)
6. a. Agabus (Acts 11:28)
7. False; Antioch Christians sent the relief (Acts 11:27, 29).
8. d. the Holy Ghost (Acts 13:2)
9. John, Mark (Acts 12:25)
10. Jerusalem (Acts 15:2)
11. True (Acts 15:10)
12. b. James (Acts 15:13, 19)
13. Blood (Acts 15:20)
14. False; Peter came to the city (Galatians 2:11).
15. False; he was persecuted in Antioch (2 Timothy 3:11).

LEG 20
WELCOME TO THE CHECK-IN MAT

Did you do well in exploring the events that occurred in Antioch? The church at Antioch became the first center of Gentile Christianity. But some disciples in Jerusalem insisted that Gentile believers must first become Jews. A delegation led by Barnabas and Paul traveled to Jerusalem to settle the matter. Peter spoke first, then Barnabas and Paul. They strongly championed the idea that the Gospel is for everyone. Then James presented his views.

Many scholars believe James was a brother of Jesus and the leader of the ultra-orthodox group of Jewish Christians in Jerusalem. Perhaps the Jewish-leaning believers thought he would agree with them. But he, too, declared that observing the Law of Moses was not necessary for Gentile Christians to be accepted with God.

Even before that decision, Paul had begun his work among Gentiles. During his first missionary journey, he traveled the sixteen miles from Antioch to the Mediterranean Sea and then sailed to a large island off the coast of Syria. That is your next destination as well.

> . . . .*and of all the heathen, which are*
> *called by my name, saith the Lord.*
> AMOS 9:12

LEG 21

Good morning. Time to wake up and make ready for the next challenge. The rest of the contestants are preparing, too. Success will require knowledge of Paul's first missionary journey. There's the clue box. Check for the next amazing place. Godspeed.

Clue Box:

As Barnabas, Paul, and John Mark leave Antioch, their first destination is an island that is the birthplace of Barnabas. You will travel to the island and follow Paul as he teaches the deputy of the island. It is here that Saul is henceforth called Paul, a name he shared with the deputy of the island, Sergius Paulus. Paul also confronts a sorcerer. You, too, will be challenged to answer questions about sorcerers, magicians, and witches in the Old Testament.

Sail to the island of _____.

What was the name of the sorcerer who withstood Barnabas and Paul at Paphos on Cyprus?

    a.   Barjesus, or Elymas by interpretation
    b.   Belteshazzar
    c.   Lucius
    d.   Seleucia

Paul said the hand of the Lord would bring _____ on the sorcerer at Paphos.

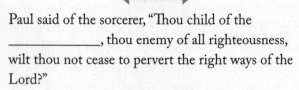

Paul said of the sorcerer, "Thou child of the _____, thou enemy of all righteousness, wilt thou not cease to pervert the right ways of the Lord?"

True or False: The deputy of the island, Sergius Paulus, became a believer.

True or False: John Mark stayed on the island of Cyprus to preach.

True or False: In Genesis, Pharaoh commanded his magicians to interpret his dream without telling it to them.

In addition to fat and lean cattle (kine), what other fat and lean things did Pharaoh dream about?

True or False: Joseph was in prison (a dungeon) when called upon to interpret Pharaoh's dream.

What did Joseph tell Pharaoh the "seven" in the dream meant?

a. seven abundant and seven lean years
b. seven strong and weak kingdoms
c. the number of days before disaster befell Pharaoh
d. the seven treasure cities of Egypt

In Exodus, the one who acted as spokesman in telling Pharaoh to let God's people go was:

a. Aaron
b. Moses

How did God demonstrate that the serpent from Aaron's rod had greater power than serpents from the rods of the magicians of Pharaoh?

Who in the Old Testament consulted the Witch of Endor (the woman who had a familiar spirit) to ask Samuel what to do about the Philistines?

In the Old Testament book of Daniel, why did Nebuchadnezzar not tell his dream to his magicians, astrologers, and sorcerers?

a. Daniel told him not to do so.
b. God required his soul before he could tell them.
c. He could not remember it.
d. He wanted to test them.

The head of the image in Nebuchadnezzar's dream was made of what metal?

The legs of the image were made of iron, and "his feet part of iron and part of _____."

LEG 21
ANSWERS

Cyprus

1. a. Barjesus, or Elymas by interpretation (Acts 13:6, 8)
2. Blindness (Acts 13:11)
3. Devil (Acts 13:10)
4. True (Acts 13:12)
5. False; he traveled a while longer with Paul and Barnabas (Acts 13:13).
6. False; he did describe it (Genesis 41:8).
7. Ears (of grain) (Genesis 41:22–23)
8. True (Genesis 41:14)
9. a. seven abundant and seven lean years (Genesis 41:26–27)
10. a. Aaron (Exodus 7:2)
11. It swallowed them (Exodus 7:12).
12. King Saul (1 Samuel 28:7, 11, 15)
13. c. He could not remember it (Daniel 2:4–5).
14. Gold (Daniel 2:32)
15. Clay (Daniel 2:33)

LEG 21
WELCOME TO THE CHECK-IN MAT

Did you answer at least twelve questions correctly? Good for you. Whether you answered twelve or two, take time to rest, enjoy good food, and discuss this difficult leg with the other contestants. Then prepare for the next leg, which will continue to follow Paul.

Although Paul found his greatest success as a missionary to the Gentiles, he did not turn to them exclusively. He always approached the local synagogue first. He gave the Jews every opportunity to embrace Jesus. But when they rejected Him, he turned to the Gentiles.

Prepare now to follow Paul and Barnabas as they continue on their one-thousand-mile first missionary journey.

Blessed be the name of God for ever and ever:
for wisdom and might are his:
And he changeth the times and the seasons:
he removeth kings, and setteth up kings:
he giveth wisdom unto the wise,
and knowledge to them that know understanding.
DANIEL 2:20–21

THAT AMAZING
PLACE

LEG 22

Your next challenge will begin shortly. Like Paul, you will leave Cyprus, sail to the mainland of Asia Minor, and travel overland. Your destination is a city where Paul was well received at first. But his enemies rallied opposition. They stoned him and carried him for dead outside the city. There's the clue box. Check where you are going to next.

CLUE BOX:

This amazing place is a city where Paul did a notable miracle. Local people tried to offer sacrifices to Paul and Barnabas, and worship them as gods. It is also in this town that a young disciple lived. Later, two of Paul's letters to him would become books of the New Testament.

Race to _____.

1.

When threatened with stoning in Iconium, Paul and Barnabas traveled to Lystra and what other city near Lystra?

a. Corinth
b. Derbe
c. Paphos
d. Philippi

2.

What miracle did Paul do while in Lystra?

a. He called down fire to consume a pagan sacrifice.
b. He drove evil spirits out of a servant girl.
c. He healed a man born blind.
d. He healed a man lame from his mother's womb.

3.

After Paul's miracle, the people said, "The gods are come down to us in the likeness of _____."

Why did the people of Lystra call Paul Mercurius (Mercury)?

What name did the people of Lystra give to Barnabas?

a. Adonijah of Cyprus
b. Jupiter
c. Mars
d. Odin the Wanderer

True or False: Paul was unable to restrain the people from sacrificing to him and Barnabas.

True or False: After being stoned and left for dead outside of Lystra, Paul never again returned to that city.

When Paul and Barnabas decided to revisit the churches where they had preached, why did Paul think it not good to take John Mark?

True or False: John Mark was related to Barnabas.

Rather than John Mark, who was Paul's traveling companion?

Timothy's father was a:

    a. Greek
    b. Jew

The name of Timothy's mother was Eunice; what was the name of his grandmother?

13.

Later, what did Paul say about John Mark when writing to Timothy?

a. "Beware, lest he betray you."
b. "He has a form of godliness, but denies the power thereof."
c. "He is a man after mine own heart."
d. "He is profitable to me for the ministry."

14.

Paul wrote to Timothy that in the last days men shall be "_____ of pleasures more than _____ of God." (same word)

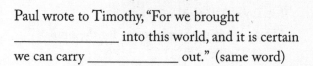

15.

Paul wrote to Timothy, "For we brought _____ into this world, and it is certain we can carry _____ out." (same word)

LEG 22
ANSWERS

Lystra

1. b. Derbe (Acts 14:6)
2. d. He healed a man lame from his mother's womb (Acts 14:8, 10).
3. Men (Acts 14:11)
4. He was the chief speaker (Acts 14:12).
5. b. Jupiter (Acts 14:12)
6. False; he did restrain them (Acts 14:18).
7. False; he did return (Acts 14:20–21, 16:1).
8. He had departed from them (Acts 15:38).
9. True; his nephew (Colossians 4:10)
10. Silas (Acts 15:40)
11. a. Greek (Acts16:1)
12. Lois (2 Timothy 1:5)
13. d. "He is profitable to me for the ministry" (2 Timothy 4:11).
14. Lovers (2 Timothy 3:4)
15. Nothing (1 Timothy 6:7)

LEG 22
WELCOME TO THE CHECK-IN MAT

How did you do on this leg? Did you come in first? Winning a race requires endurance. Paul certainly showed perseverance. After being stoned in Lystra, he walked back into the city that night. He visited it again as he backtracked his route from Derbe. Later, on the second missionary journey, he once again preached in the city where he previously had been stoned. Following the Lord's will takes courage. But God protects His servants to accomplish His purposes.

Soon, you will be racing again. The next city is one Paul, Silas, and Timothy traveled to on the second missionary journey.

Now therefore fear the Lord,
and serve him in sincerity and in truth:
and put away the gods which your fathers served
on the other side of the flood, and in Egypt;
and serve ye the Lord.
JOSHUA 24:14

LEG 23

Congratulations. You've made it this far. Look! I see the rest of the contestants are making ready. It's time to continue. After Paul and Silas visited Lystra a second time, Timothy began traveling with them. They traveled east to Troas, where Luke is likely to have joined them. They took a ship across the Aegean Sea to Neapolis and then to their (and your) next destination. Paul was now closer to the heart of the Roman Empire than he was to Jerusalem.

Clue Box:

In this city Paul preached to a group of women who were holding a prayer service. He converted a businesswoman and her household to Christianity, and freed a young maiden from a spirit of divination. He and Silas spent a night in jail, and the jailer himself became a Christian. Later, Paul wrote a letter that became a book of the New Testament to the Christians in this city.

Race to _____.

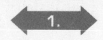

Philippi was the chief city of what colony?

a. Cappadocia
b. Cyrenia
c. Macedonia
d. Pontus

What caused Paul to leave Troas and go to Philippi?

At Philippi, where did Paul find Lydia and the women praying?

a. by the river side
b. in her home
c. in the marketplace
d. in the women's court of the Synagogue

Lydia was from:

   a. Philippi
   b. Thyatira

What was Lydia's profession?

The damsel possessed with a spirit said, "These men are the servants of the most high God, which shew unto us the way of _____."

Why were the masters of the damsel upset because Paul had freed her of the spirit of divination?

True or False: The city magistrates threw Paul and Silas into prison to await a trial the next day.

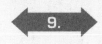

What time did the prisoners hear Paul and Silas praying and singing praises unto God?

How were the doors of the prison opened?

a. by an angel of the Lord
b. by an earthquake
c. by the jailer
d. The doors opened and chains fell away with no visible cause.

What did the jailer plan on doing when he found the prison doors open?

a. call for the sergeants and Roman guards
b. kill himself with a sword
c. offer sacrifices to his household gods
d. say that the disciples had secretly released them at night

When the jailer found none of the prisoners had escaped, he said "Sirs, what must I do to be _____?"

True or False: Both Lydia and the jailer were baptized.

In his letter to the Philippians, Paul wrote, "I can do all things through Christ which _____ me."

In his letter to the Philippians, Paul wrote, "_____ in the Lord always: and again I say, _____." (same word)

LEG 23
ANSWERS

Philippi

1. c. Macedonia (Acts 16:12)
2. The vision of a man from Macedonia (Acts 16:7–9)
3. a. by the river side (Acts 16:13)
4. b. Thyatira (Acts 16:14)
5. Seller of purple (Acts 16:14)
6. Salvation (Acts 16:17)
7. Their hope of gains was gone (Acts 16:19).
8. False; they beat Paul and Silas without a trial (Acts 16:22–23).
9. Midnight (Acts 16:25)
10. b. by an earthquake (Acts 16:26)
11. b. kill himself with a sword (Acts 16:27)
12. Saved (Acts 16:30)
13. True (Acts 16:15, 33)
14. Strengtheneth (Philippians 4:13)
15. Rejoice (Philippians 4:4)

LEG 23
WELCOME TO THE CHECK-IN MAT

When we travel, we like to keep in touch with family and friends. Paul did, too, although he didn't have the instant communication of e-mail. Instead, he depended on friends or trusted travelers to deliver messages. One of the wonderful things about the Philippians is that they kept in touch with Paul. They sent him a gift (Philippians 4:18) during a time when he felt so many others had abandoned him. He responded to their warm affection with a letter to them that became the book of Philippians.

Paul had already been stoned in a Roman city (Lystra), beaten and jailed in another (Philippi), and his route was taking him ever closer to Rome itself. But with the conversion of Lydia, he pressed ahead despite the danger. At the next amazing place, he encountered threats even more severe than those in Philippi.

Finally, brethren, whatsoever things are true,
whatsoever things are honest, whatsoever things are just,
whatsoever things are pure, whatsoever things are lovely,
whatsoever things are of good report; if there be any
virtue, and if there be any praise, think on these things.
PHILIPPIANS 4:8

Facing the challenge of each amazing place takes fortitude. Paul bravely accepted each new challenge. How did he do it? In his letter to the Philippians he said, "I can do all things through Christ which strengtheneth me" (Philippians 4:13).

Follow Paul as he travels southwest to a city that is about ninety miles from Philippi. Located on a north-western inlet of the Aegean Sea, it is one of the most important and best-known Greek cities. Here, Paul preaches first to the Jews. He tells them that Jesus is the Christ (that is, the Messiah). He carries the same message to the Greeks and many believe. Open the clue box for more information about your destination.

CLUE BOX:

In this city, the Jewish leaders who did not believe stormed the house where they thought Paul was staying. Although Paul was not there, the mob carried the home's owner before the rulers of the city and made false charges against him. To calm the situation, Paul left the city after a brief stay. Later, Paul learned that Gentile believers in the city were struggling to remain faithful. Paul wrote them a letter to encourage them. That letter and a second one became two of the books of the New Testament.

Travel to the Greek city of _____.

In Thessalonica, Paul spoke in a:

    a.   Greek temple
    b.   Jewish synagogue

"Christ must needs have _____, and risen again from the dead."

Of the prominent Greek women in Thessalonica:

    a.   only a few believed
    b.   not a few believed

What emotion moved the unbelieving Jews to oppose Paul?

To whose house did the enemies of Paul come in search of him?

a. Demas
b. Jason
c. Philemon
d. Titus

The unbelieving Jews said Paul had acted against whose decrees?

How did the ones taken before the rulers of the city avoid spending the night in jail?

Compared to the Jews in the synagogue at Thessalonica, those in the synagogue of Berea could be called what?

a. friends of God
b. noble searchers of scripture
c. peacemakers
d. without superstition

9.

True or False: As Paul preached in Thessalonica and Berea, Greek men became believers in both cities.

10.

Who came from Thessalonica to Berea and stirred up trouble?

   a. magistrates
   b. Roman soldiers
   c. unbelieving Jews
   d. worshippers of the goddess Diana

11.

True or False: After those from Thessalonica stirred up trouble in Berea, Paul sent Silas and Timothy on ahead to safety.

12.

Who were the ones who sent a gift to Paul in Thessalonica?

   a. believers in Jerusalem
   b. his friends in Antioch
   c. Titus and Luke who had returned to Troas
   d. Christians in Philippi

Later, when writing to Timothy, who did Paul say had forsaken him and loved "this present world" and had departed to Thessalonica?

   a. Demas
   b. John Mark
   c. Onesimus
   d. Titus

In a letter to the Thessalonians, Paul wrote, "For the Lord himself shall descend from heaven with a shout, with the voice of the _____, and with the trump of God: and the dead in Christ shall rise first."

Paul wrote to the Thessalonians about the Wicked one "whose coming is after the working of Satan with all power and signs and _____ wonders."

LEG 24
ANSWERS

Thessalonica

1. b. a Jewish synagogue (Acts 17:1–2)
2. Suffered (Acts 17:3)
3. b. not a few (Acts 17:4)
4. Envy (Acts 17:5)
5. b. Jason (Acts 17:5)
6. Caesar (Acts 17:7)
7. They put up security (bail) (Acts 17:9).
8. b. noble searchers of scripture (Acts 17:10–11)
9. True (Acts 17:4, 12)
10. c. unbelieving Jews (Acts 17:13)
11. False; the brethren sent away Paul (Acts 17:14).
12. d. Christians in Philippi (Philippians 4:15–17)
13. a. Demas (2 Timothy 4:10)
14. Archangel (1 Thessalonians 4:16)
15. Lying (2 Thessalonians 2:8–9)

LEG 24
WELCOME TO THE CHECK-IN MAT

How did you do? Each new amazing place brings different and more difficult challenges. Like Paul, we may be willing to put ourselves in the way of danger for some adventure, but we avoid risky actions if they threaten those we love. During the early part of Paul's ministry, he put himself at risk time and again. But as others traveled with him, he became concerned about the safety of his companions. To avoid making trouble for Jason and his friends in Thessalonica, Paul and his companions left the city.

Forty miles away, they reached Berea. There they received a warmer reception. But his enemies from Thessalonica descended on Berea, too. Rather than endanger his companions, Paul left Berea and pressed ahead alone. Paul traveled two hundred miles south to the greatest of all the Greek cities—and so will you as you race to the next amazing place.

Rejoice evermore. Pray without ceasing.
In every thing give thanks: for this is the will of God
in Christ Jesus concerning you. Quench not the Spirit.
Despise not prophesyings. Prove all things;
hold fast that which is good.
Abstain from all appearance of evil.
1 THESSALONIANS 5:16–22

THAT AMAZING
PLACE

LEG 25

Prepare for another long journey. You will travel more than two hundred miles from Thessalonica to the main city in Greece. At one time, it was the greatest city-state of the ancient world. But its glory had faded by the time Paul visited. Nevertheless, it still held first place as a center of art, literature, and philosophy. It is time to get on with the race. There is the clue box. See what it says.

CLUE BOX:

Travel to the city noted for its freedom of speech in ancient times. Paul was asked to come to the Areopagus and address the learned philosophers. They listened politely to him but dismissed his message.

Race to _____.

Paul's spirit was stirred in him because he saw Athens wholly given to what?

True or False: Athens did not have a synagogue.

In Athens, Paul taught in the marketplace:

a. on the Sabbath day
b. daily

Paul was asked to speak to the Epicureans and what other type of philosophers?

a. Agnostics
b. Pythagoreans
c. Skeptics
d. Stoicks (Stoics)

What was the name of the hill on which Paul addressed the philosophers?

Paul said that he perceived that the Athenians were too what?

    a. argumentative
    b. ignorant
    c. intolerant
    d. superstitious

Paul found an altar with this inscription, TO THE _____ GOD.

"Whom therefore ye _____ worship, him declare I unto you."

Paul told the Greek philosophers that God had made all nations of one what?

    a. blood
    b. heart
    c. mind
    d. necessity

True or False: In speaking to the philosophers of Athens, Paul quoted one of their poets.

"For in him we live, and move, and have our
_____."

Paul said that in times past God winked at what?

13.

What part of Paul's sermon caused some of the philosophers to mock?

14.

What did the philosophers tell Paul after he finished speaking?

a. They asked him to speak only to the Jews.
b. They asked him to write to them after he left.
c. They ordered him to depart.
d. They told him he would be heard again.

15.

True or False: Paul made no converts in Athens.

LEG 25
ANSWERS

Athens

1. Idolatry (Acts 17:16)
2. False (Acts 17:17)
3. b. daily (Acts 17:17)
4. d. Stoicks (Stoics) (Acts 17:18)
5. Mars' hill (Acts 17:22)
6. d. superstitious (Acts 17:22)
7. UNKNOWN (Acts 17:23)
8. Ignorantly (Acts 17:23)
9. a. blood (Acts 17:26)
10. True (Acts 17:28)
11. Being (Acts 17:28)
12. Ignorance (Acts 17:30)
13. Resurrection of the dead (Acts 17:32)
14. d. They told him he would be heard again (Acts 17:32).
15. False; Dionysius and Damaris believed (Acts 17:34).

LEG 25
WELCOME TO THE CHECK-IN MAT

Paul may have been disappointed in the number of people who became converts in Athens. Although he did not encounter hard opposition, neither did he receive an enthusiastic reception. In other cities he may have been stoned, but he also left behind disciples fervent for Christ. The New Testament has letters to the Ephesians, Galatians, and Thessalonians, but not to the Athenians. Great opposition also sometimes results in great opportunities, while a polite reception may result in a lukewarm response.

Continue now with Paul as he leaves Athens and visits a city about fifty miles to its southwest. He meets for the first time a husband and wife evangelistic team.

Hear, O my people, and I will testify unto thee:
O Israel, if thou wilt hearken unto me;
There shall no strange god be in thee;
neither shalt thou worship any strange god.
I am the Lord thy God, which brought thee
out of the land of Egypt: open thy mouth wide,
and I will fill it.
PSALM 81:8–10

LEG 26

After leaving Athens, Paul traveled to another city in Greece. The Romans had made this city, and not Athens, the capital of the Roman province that included Greece. It had become an important and prosperous city. Consult the clue box for a description of your next destination.

CLUE BOX:

In this amazing place, Paul met two people—husband and wife—who became his friends. They were missionaries, too, and even shared the same occupation as Paul. Later, Paul wrote two letters to the Christians in this city that became books of the New Testament.

Go to _____.

What country did Aquila and Priscilla leave to come to Corinth?

Who had expelled the Jews, including Aquila and Priscilla, from the city?

    a. Augustus
    b. Claudius
    c. Nero
    d. Ptolemy

What was the occupation of Paul, Aquila, and Priscilla?

When the Jews rejected Paul's teaching he said, "Your _____ be upon your own heads; I am clean."

Who was the chief ruler of the synagogue who believed on the Lord?

    a.   Apollo
    b.   Crispus
    c.   Gallio
    d.   Justus

The number of Corinthians who believed was:

    a.   few
    b.   many

True or False: In a vision, the Lord warned of a terrible harm about to overcome Paul in Corinth.

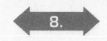

When Paul was brought before the deputy of
Arcadia, what action did the deputy take?

    a.   He avoided a trial by traveling to a far
          country.

    b.   He charged the Gentiles with creating a
          disturbance.

    c.   He referred the matter to Caesar.

    d.   He said, "I will be no judge of such
          matters."

True or False: Paul fled from Corinth after only
three weeks.

Why did Paul shave his head?

True or False: In 1 Corinthians, Paul specifically
states that the letter is to the church of God at
Corinth.

Paul tells the Corinthians that their body is the temple of whom?

For every temptation God will provide a way of

_____.

In the introduction to 2 Corinthians, whom did Paul name as also sending the letter?

  a. Barnabas
  b. John Mark
  c. Silas
  d. Timothy

In 2 Corinthians, Paul writes, "My grace is sufficient for thee: for my strength is made perfect in _____."

LEG 26
ANSWERS

Corinth

1. Italy (Acts 18:2)
2. b. Claudius (Acts 18:2)
3. Tentmakers (Acts 18:3)
4. Blood (Acts 18:6)
5. b. Crispus (Acts 18:8)
6. b. many (Acts 18:8)
7. False; no one would seek to hurt him (Acts 18:9–10).
8. d. He said, "I will be no judge of such matters" (Acts 18:15).
9. False; he stayed at least a year and six months (Acts 18:11).
10. To keep a vow (Acts 18:18)
11. True (1 Corinthians 1:2)
12. Holy Ghost (1 Corinthians 6:19)
13. Escape (1 Corinthians 10:13)
14. d. Timothy (2 Corinthians 1:1)
15. Weakness (2 Corinthians 12:9)

LEG 26
WELCOME TO THE CHECK-IN MAT

Paul arrived in Corinth shortly after Claudius had ordered the Jews from Rome. The Romans considered Christians to be merely a sect of the Jews, so any persecution of the Jews spilled over to affect Christians, too—as Aquila and Priscilla well knew.

Prepare for the next challenge because, ready or not, it is time to move on. The next amazing place is a city noted for a false goddess. The temple and statue of her were so imposing as to be considered one of the wonders of the ancient world.

Charity suffereth long, and is kind;
charity envieth not; charity vaunteth not itself,
is not puffed up, doth not behave itself unseemly,
seeketh not her own, is not easily provoked,
thinketh no evil.
1 CORINTHIANS 13:4–5

THAT AMAZING
PLACE

LEG 27

When Paul left Corinth, he and Aquila and Priscilla sailed east 250 miles across the Aegean Sea to the coast of Asia Minor. In this city some Jewish exorcists tried to drive out evil spirits as Paul did, but had to flee as the spirits attacked them. For seven hundred years, the city was the destination of pagans who worshipped at a temple in the city. The temple covered acres of land and those worshipping the false goddess arrived by walking along a marble highway.

CLUE BOX:

In your next destination, Paul convinced people of the folly of worshipping an idol made with human hands. He became so successful that those who sold models of the goddess became concerned their business would suffer and tried to silence him.

Go to _____.

The first time Paul visited Ephesus, he hurried away to keep a feast in what city?

Apollos, the eloquent Jew who came to Ephesus, had been born in what city?

    a. Alexandria
    b. Athens
    c. Philadelphia
    d. Syrene

True or False: Apollos explained more clearly the word of God to Aquila and Priscilla.

In Ephesus, Paul found believers who had not heard of the _____ _____. (two words)

Paul said that John baptized with the baptism of
_____.

When those in the synagogue at Ephesus rejected
Paul, he disputed daily in whose school?

   a. Gamalial
   b. Sophocles
   c. Tychicus
   d. Tyrannus

Sceva had how many sons who tried to drive out
evil spirits?

The evil spirits said, "_____ I know, and
_____ I know; but who are ye?"

What did the believers do to their books of "curious arts?"

    a.   burned them
    b.   hid them from sight
    c.   sold them and gave the money to Paul
    d.   tore up the books and threw them to the
       wind

What was the name of the goddess that had a statue in Ephesus?

What was the profession of Demetrius who opposed Paul at Ephesus?

The town clerk urged the people in the theater to:

a. Put Paul in chains.
b. Do nothing rashly.

True or False: Paul wrote two letters to the Ephesians that became books of the New Testament.

True or False: In Revelation, Ephesus is identified as one of the seven churches of Asia.

Paul writes to the Ephesians and tells them, "And he gave some, apostles; and some, prophets; and some, evangelists; and some, pastors and _____."

LEG 27
ANSWERS

Ephesus

1. Jerusalem (Acts 18:21)
2. a. Alexandria (Acts 18:24)
3. False; they expounded the way of God more perfectly to Apollos (Acts 18:26).
4. Holy Ghost (Acts 19:2)
5. Repentance (Acts 19:4)
6. d. Tyrannus (Acts 19:9)
7. Seven (Acts 19:13–14)
8. Jesus, Paul (Acts 19:15)
9. a. burned them (Acts 19:19)
10. Diana (Acts 19:24–28)
11. Silversmith (Acts 19:24)
12. b. Do nothing rashly (Acts 19:35–36).
13. False; only one (Ephesians 1:1)
14. True (Revelation 1:11)
15. Teachers (Ephesians 4:11)

LEG 27
WELCOME TO THE CHECK-IN MAT

Ephesus is where the second missionary journey of Paul ended. He made a quick trip back to Jerusalem (Acts 19:21) and then returned to Ephesus on his third missionary journey. In retracing his steps, you can gather strength by thinking upon the Bible verse at the end of each leg. Take a rest, get some sleep, and wake up tomorrow refreshed and ready to race again.

You are about to embark on an exciting voyage along the Mediterranean Sea to an island where Paul and other shipwreck victims manage to swim ashore after a terrific storm that destroyed the ship in which they sailed.

For by grace are ye saved through faith;
and that not of yourselves: it is the gift of God:
Not of works, lest any man should boast.
Ephesians 2:8–9

THAT AMAZING
PLACE

LEG 28

Paul completed his third missionary journey and returned to Jerusalem where he once again faced a deadly situation. He was arrested and taken to Caesarea to stand trial. But as a Roman citizen, he had the right to be judged by Caesar. Under guard, Paul sailed across the Mediterranean Sea in what became a fourth missionary trip. Paul's life had been filled with exciting adventures, but seldom does the story come alive as much as the events surrounding the storm and shipwreck. Read the clue to discover your next amazing place.

Clue Box:

The captain of the ship Paul was aboard delayed seeking a safe harbor and became swept up in a terrific storm that lasted for two weeks. Despite the sailors' efforts, the ship broke apart. Paul, the other prisoners, soldiers, and sailors struggled ashore while the storm still raged. On the island, the inhabitants watched closely after a serpent bit Paul. They thought he would surely die.

Sail to the island of _____.

True or False: The soldier charged with taking Paul to Italy was a centurion.

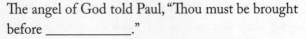

Before the shipwreck at Melita, Paul said, "For there stood by me this night the angel of God, whose I am, and whom I _____."

The angel of God told Paul, "Thou must be brought before _____."

After taking soundings, what did the shipmen fear?

    a. The storm was growing stronger.
    b. They were in a whirlpool.
    c. They were in deep water.
    d. They were near rocks.

On the fourteenth day of the storm, Paul urged those aboard the ship to:

a. fast
b. take food

How many people were aboard the ship that was destroyed by the storm?

a. about a dozen
b. between fifty and sixty
c. between two hundred and three hundred
d. more than five hundred

"And the _____s' counsel was to kill the prisoners, lest any of them should swim out, and escape."

True or False: Everyone aboard the ship could swim.

True or False: The barbarous people of Melita attacked Paul and the other shipwreck victims.

What was the weather like when the shipwreck victims came ashore on Melita?

Where had Paul put the bundle of sticks when the viper bit him?

What did the people of Melita say about Paul when the viper bit him?

How did Paul kill the viper?

a. He commanded it to die.
b. He crushed its head with his foot.
c. He shook it off into the fire.
d. He turned it into a wooden stake.

What did the people say about Paul when he showed no ill effects of the viper bite?

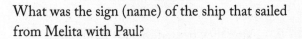

What was the sign (name) of the ship that sailed from Melita with Paul?

a. Castor and Pollux
b. Euroclydon
c. Fair Havens
d. Three Eagles

LEG 28
ANSWERS

Melita

1. True (Acts 27:1)
2. Serve (Acts 27:23)
3. Caesar (Acts 27:24)
4. d. They were near rocks (Acts 27:28–29).
5. b. take food (Acts 27:33–34)
6. c. between two hundred and three hundred (Acts 27:37)
7. Soldier (Acts 27:42)
8. False; some could not swim (Acts 27:43–44).
9. False; they treated them with kindness (Acts 28:2).
10. Cold and rainy (Acts 28:2)
11. Laid them on the fire (Acts 28:3)
12. This man is a murderer (Acts 18:4).
13. c. He shook it off into the fire (Acts 28:5).
14. He was a god (Acts 28:6).
15. a. Castor and Pollux (Acts 28:11)

LEG 28
WELCOME TO THE CHECK-IN MAT

Those who enjoy tracing out Paul's journeys still visit the island of Malta (Melita) today. But more important than following his physical route is making the spiritual journey to arrive at a closer relationship with the Savior. If your scores on the legs have not been as you would want them to be, then reset your knowledge by using the verses given in the answers as a guide to reading the Bible.

The race continues. For Paul it is the place where he would stand trial. You will be going there, too.

I am crucified with Christ: nevertheless I live;
yet not I, but Christ liveth in me: and the life
which I now live in the flesh I live by the faith of the
Son of God, who loved me, and gave himself for me.
GALATIANS 2:20

LEG 29

When Paul arrived in this city to stand trial, it was a great and prosperous city. It was the capital of an empire that extended west to Portugal, east to Babylon, south to Africa, and north to England. Due to capable leadership at the middle level, the Empire enjoyed influence and affluence. Such dedicated government officials included men like Cornelius, the town clerk at Ephesus, and the Roman captain who rescued Paul at the temple in Jerusalem. Citizens of the Empire were less fortunate than their leaders at the top. They had suffered through years of rule by wasteful and pleasure-loving emperors.

Clue Box:

This is the city where Paul was to stand trial. Like trials today, it was not over quickly. But the delay was not idle time for Paul. He wrote letters, converted some of Caesar's own household to Christianity, and received visitors. Paul's book written to the people of this city details a thorough and concise explanation of the Gospel.

Race to the city of _____.

True or False: People from Rome heard Peter speak in Jerusalem on the day of Pentecost.

True or False: The believers in Rome came out to meet Paul before he arrived in that city.

In Rome, Paul was allowed to live by himself with a _____ that kept him.

True or False: The Jews in Rome refused to listen to Paul.

What did the Jewish leaders in Rome say about followers of Jesus Christ?

     a. They had heard nothing about them.
     b. They were every where spoken against.
     c. They were found only among the barbarians.
     d. They were well regarded.

True or False: Some people in Rome believed what Paul said.

What Old Testament prophet was Paul quoting to the Romans when he said, "For the heart of this people is waxed gross"?

At the end of Acts, Paul had been in Rome for how long?

a. three months
b. two years
c. five years
d. until his death

Where did Paul stay while in Rome?

a. at a place called the Three Taverns
b. in a hired house
c. in prison
d. in the home of a believing Jew

10.

How did Paul address those to whom he wrote the book of Romans?

    a.   strangers in Rome

    b.   to all that be in Rome, beloved of God, called to be saints

    c.   to all the brethren in Rome who suffer with me

    d.   to the church of God in Rome, sanctified in Christ Jesus

11.

In the book of Romans, Paul wrote, "For I am not _____ of the gospel of Christ: for it is the power of God unto salvation to every one that believeth."

12.

Who diligently sought out Paul in Rome?

    a.   Aquila and Priscilla

    b.   Onesiphorus

    c.   Philemon

    d.   Timothy

What have all done to come short of the glory of God?

"What shall we say then? Shall we continue in sin, that _____ may abound?"

"So then faith cometh by _____, and _____ by the word of God." (same word)

LEG 29
ANSWERS

Rome

1. True (Acts 2:1, 10)
2. True (Acts 28:14–15)
3. Soldier (Acts 28:16)
4. False; they did ask to hear him (Acts 28:17, 22).
5. b. They were every where spoken against (Acts 28:22).
6. True (Acts 28:24)
7. Esaias (Isaiah) (Acts 28:25–27)
8. b. two years (Acts 28:30)
9. b. in a hired house (Acts 28:30)
10. b. to all that be in Rome, beloved of God, called to be saints (Romans 1:7)
11. Ashamed (Romans 1:16)
12. b. Onesiphorus (2 Timothy 1:16–17)
13. Sinned (Romans 3:23)
14. Grace (Romans 6:1)
15. Hearing (Romans 10:17)

LEG 29
WELCOME TO THE CHECK-IN MAT

Acts ends with Paul still awaiting trial. At times he felt lonely and said so in his letters: "At my first answer no man stood with me, but all men forsook me" (2 Timothy 4:16). But he also had a sense of triumph and of a mission fulfilled: "I have fought a good fight, I have finished my course, I have kept the faith" (2 Timothy 4:7). Acts ends with the chief apostle to the Gentiles at the chief city of the Gentile world.

After the hustle and bustle of Rome, prepare now for a visit to a nearly uninhabited and desolate island in the Aegean Sea. Take new courage because the end is in sight—the next leg takes you to the last amazing place.

I beseech you therefore, brethren, by the mercies of God,
that ye present your bodies a living sacrifice, holy,
acceptable unto God, which is your reasonable service.
And be not conformed to this world:
but be ye transformed by the renewing of your mind,
that ye may prove what is that good,
and acceptable, and perfect, will of God.

ROMANS 12:1-2

THAT AMAZING
PLACE

LEG 30

This is your last amazing place, and the final check-in will be at the end of this leg. Travel to a small, rocky island off the coast of Asia Minor, about seventy miles southwest of Ephesus. Here John, under the direction of Jesus, wrote letters to seven churches located in Asia Minor, a region controlled by the Romans. Living as Christians in these pagan cities must have been difficult. The early Christians fell prey to the ways of the pagan world. The letters sent to the seven churches clearly told them where they had fallen short—but blessed them when they managed to stay faithful despite the desolate pagan life and idol worship all around them.

CLUE BOX:

Your destination is an isle mentioned in the last book of the New Testament. The title of the book comes from its first line: The Revelation of Jesus Christ. The isle is where John wrote what he saw and sent letters to the seven churches.

Go to _____.

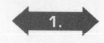

True or False: John describes his reason for being on the isle of Patmos as being "in exile as a prophet called Faithful and True."

What phrase does the Almighty use to signify that He is the beginning and the ending?

"Unto him that loved us, and washed us from our sins in his own _____, . . .to him be glory and dominion for ever and ever."

Which of the seven churches of Asia is missing from this list: Ephesus, Smyrna, Pergamos, Thyatira, Sardis, and Laodicea.

True or False: The one like unto the Son of man had hair that glowed as polished brass.

What went out of the mouth of the one like unto the Son of man?

a. flames of fire
b. seven stars
c. smoke and glowing embers
d. twoedged sword

Who had the keys of hell and death?

a. Balaam
b. Satan
c. the morning star
d. the one like unto the Son of man

The seven churches are represented by seven:

a. stars
b. candlesticks

True or False: The phrase "thou hast left thy first love" was addressed to three of the seven churches of Asia.

To Smyrna, John was told to write, "Be thou faithful unto death, and I will give thee a _____ of life."

True or False: The phrase "which thing I hate" was applied to the doctrine of Nicolaitanes.

What temperature is used to describe the
Laodiceans?

"Behold, I stand at the door, and _____:
if any man hear my voice, and open the door, I will
come in to him, and will sup with him, and he with
me."

In Revelation, what was the color of the horse being
ridden by death?

"And I saw a new _____ and a
new_____: for the first _____
and the first _____ were passed away; and
there was no more sea." (two words, repeated)

LEG 30
ANSWERS

Patmos

1. False; he does not call himself "Faithful and True" (Revelation 1:9; 19:11).
2. "I am Alpha and Omega" (Revelation 1:8).
3. Blood (Revelation 1:5–6)
4. Philadelphia (Revelation 1:11)
5. False; white like wool (Revelation 1:14)
6. d. twoedged sword (Revelation 1:16)
7. d. the one like unto the Son of man (Revelation 1:13, 18)
8. b. candlesticks (Revelation 1:20)
9. False; only Ephesus (Revelation 2:1, 4)
10. Crown (Revelation 2:8, 10)
11. True (Revelation 2:15)
12. Lukewarm, or neither cold nor hot (Revelation 3:14–16)
13. Knock (Revelation 3:20)
14. Pale (Revelation 6:8)
15. Heaven, earth, heaven, earth (Revelation 21:1)

LEG 30
WELCOME TO THE CHECK-IN MAT

Congratulations! You've checked in at all thirty Amazing Places. You've successfully followed the route markers of this challenging course. By answering the questions along each leg, you have learned much about life in the time of Jesus and others who walked many of the same roads that are still traveled today. Like the travels in this book, during life's journey, you'll face speed bumps, roadblocks, and choices at intersections. The Bible will keep you on the right spiritual path.

Although this is the final amazing place in this book, still more amazing places remain to be explored in the Bible. Read the Bible and take time to reflect on what you read. It can change your life, too. Learning more about God's love will richly reward you.

I beheld till the thrones were cast down,
and the Ancient of days did sit,
whose garment was white as snow,
and the hair of his head like the pure wool:
his throne was like the fiery flame,
and his wheels as burning fire.
DANIEL 7:9

ABOUT THE AUTHOR

John Hudson Tiner, formerly a science teacher and cartographer (mapmaker), is a freelance writer from Missouri. He is best known for his popular works on science and religion, though he has written in many genres. John and his wife, Jeanene, have two children and eight grandchildren.

Also from
Barbour Publishing

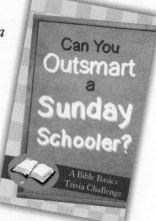

*Can You Outsmart a
Sunday Schooler?*

How well do you
remember your Bible
stories? Find out with
this new trivia challenge!
In fifty ten-question
quizzes, you'll be pressed
to recall details of the Days of Creation...
Joshua's Battle at Jericho...the Miracles of Jesus...
the Journeys of Paul...and much, much more!
Get eight to ten correct on a quiz, and you've
outsmarted the Sunday schoolers...five to seven
correct, and you must still be in Sunday school...
four or fewer, and you need to *get* to Sunday school!

ISBN 978-1-61626-024-8
4.1875" x 6.875" / 256 pages

Available wherever Christian books are sold.